# THE MONKEY THEORY

## CONQUER YOUR MENTAL CHATTER

---

SFURTI SAHARE



EBD

EMBASSY BOOKS

www.embassybooks.in

This edition Published in 2023 by:
Embassy Book Distributors 120, Great Western Building,
Maharashtra Chamber of Commerce Lane, Fort,
Mumbai 400023
Tel: (91-22) 26689026 / 26689290
Email: info@embassybooks.in
Website: www.embassybooks.in

Distribution Centres:

Mumbai, Ahmedabad, Bangalore, Kolkata, Chennai, Hyderabad, New Delhi, Pune



ISBN: 978-93-92217-75-3

Cover Design by: Sonal Churi

Printed and bound in India by Repro India Ltd., India

# Contents

# Foreword

Be it sports, or be it anything in life ... everything boils down to how you handle your idle time (the free time between two balls, innings etc.).

The time between two balls in cricket, the time between two shots in shooting or the time a person spends idle dictates how he will perform.

What happens generally is that what your mind tells you in your free time, defines your complete story in cricket or for that matter in life. The mental chatter, or in Sfurti's words: Monkey Talk!

Sometime ago, I happened to speak to a few champion sportsmen of India and they also recognised the impact this negative mental chatter has on performance .

In sports, especially in cricket, a game lasts for eight to ten hours (five days in case of a Test match), so keeping all these voices (the monkey chatter) aligned to the target determines how you perform. For instance, if a fielder drops a catch, suddenly the negative monkeys start telling him that he will drop the next one too! Similarly, if a batsmen has been bowled out by a particular bowler thrice previously, the Fear Monkey or the Judgement Monkey starts raising an alarm that this time too he will get out when that bowler bowls. If a batsmen is playing well and if he plays four balls without scoring or if he can't hit well, the negative monkeys start telling him that he is not good enough.

On top of that, a cricketer starts getting worried about the impact of a dropped catch or a mistimed six on Twitter and wonders if people have already started trolling him!

There is a lot happening in the world that is unpredictable. The dynamic nature of the game has an impact on a person's career. Today, news channels and social media has become so powerful that the slightest mistake can cost one a great deal. Therefore, cricketers have to be very tough mentally. When a cricketer scores a 100, he feels on the top of the world and the media also makes him out to be the king. When he scores badly, he feels demotivated or in fact even if he scores a 100, but in 120 balls, people are ready to troll him calling slow and selfish. This is an acid test for him.

Hence, being mentally tough and to keep the negative monkeys at bay is the key!

As with cricket, so with life.

This book helps a person to understand those voices within our head and deal with them one by one. This book is a creative tool to teach you how you can control this monkey chatter and channelise your attention in the right direction.

Today, more than motivation, young people lack focus. With technology erupting and the world becoming a small place, it's very easy to get distracted and confused.

This book helps you recognise the different forms of monkeys in your head. I could relate to the P-Monkey and his way of tricking people to avoid the gym. Similarly, how the Monkey paralyses your vision and keeps you away from thinking clearly also struck a chord with me. The metaphor of the Purple Island is brilliant and I think one should follow the complete sequence of the book to understand it better.

My experience with many international cricketers tells me that the topmost can handle their wild monkeys very well. For instance, M.S. Dhoni's biggest quality is that he is not afraid of anything and when you are not afraid, these negative voices cannot disturb you. They cannot fool you and take your attention away. And with this focused mind you can just follow the process and become good at what you do. That's why he is the master of handling pressure and is regarded as one of the best finishers in the world.

The principles and solutions given in the book are awesome. Do read, label your monkeys and get the maximum out of it.

Happy Reading!

DEEP DASGUPTA<br>Former International Cricketer and TV Presenter

# Introduction

In 2016, I published my first book—*Think and Win Like Dhoni*. Originally, I had not set out to write a book on M.S. Dhoni. I only wanted to learn from him and emulate him. Our backgrounds were similar—we both belonged to a Tier-II city, had a simple middle-class upbringing, our parents' biggest concern was that we land a 'secure' job and so on. In my case, another thing that figured prominently in my parents' list of worries was my marriage.

Like Dhoni, I too had big dreams and as time passed, I found that I was not in concurrence with my parents' version of how my life should be. I wanted to be more than a computer engineer. I wanted to pursue my dreams, grow as an individual and experience that adrenaline rush.

After reading all that was available on Dhoni in books, magazines and the internet, I finally wanted to meet him. Why? Because I felt there was more to him than just cricket. And I wanted to crack that code of 'being more'.

When I met him and spent some time with him, I got a glimpse of what Mahi was, beyond the cricket ground. His walk, his talk, the way he carried himself, the way he attentively listened to me, even though I was then a nobody—all of it was overwhelming. He had 'winner' written all over him. He was not just a cricketing star, but a phenomenon. He was a winner in life and how he had managed to do that was what I wanted to learn.

My experience was so mind-blowing that I could not keep it to myself. I had to talk about him, tell people that he was more than his wicket-keeping, more than the runs he makes and more than all the trophies he wins. He was a winner. A finisher. And I had to tell people what made him that. To decode Mahi was my goal. All of this finally shaped up into *Think and Win Like Dhoni.*

The book was an outstanding success.

The book also brought me into contact with a number of young people who read the book, believed in it, believed in me and wanted to make a difference to the world through their lives.

Much of *Think and Win like Dhoni* dealt with staying calm under pressure, being disciplined and not losing one's cool. Many readers wrote to me about things that they had noticed about themselves after reading the book. While some people said that they were easily able to control their anger, emotions, mood swings and so on, a number of others also said that in spite of being aware of the importance of being calm, they were unable to control their anger. That despite knowing the value of discipline, they were unable to tame their indiscipline; that regardless of the knowledge that smoking kills, they just could not resist the temptation; and even though they knew that getting up early was good, they could not manage to get out of their cosy beds.

Another thing I noticed was that all kinds of people seemed to be suffering a great deal. The wealthy suffered for want of meaningful relationships and difficulties at work. The middle-class were forever aspiring to climb up the ladder of success and that was a cause of suffering for them. The poor were, more often than not, beset with monetary difficulties.

That brought me to my next research topic: What is the cause of all suffering? What could be done to reduce suffering, I wondered. During my research, I came across one of the most profound thinkers of all time—Gautam Buddha. The Buddha has given the world great wisdom on avoiding suffering in a simple and straightforward manner.

One thing that he said particularly struck me. In one of his discourses, Buddha described the human mind as being filled with monkeys that were jumping around, screeching, chattering, and carrying on endlessly. It seemed to me that they were like the toughest roommates one could ever have and that too for a lifetime!

Have you chosen something only to switch to something else almost immediately? Decided to do something and ended up doing something completely different minutes later? Have you been plagued by indecision? Our choices change, our moods swing, our decisions keep fluctuating and there is a continuous mental battle going on within us.

Why does it happen?

The answers to these questions can be found in the words of the Buddha. As previously stated, the Buddha held that the human mind was filled with monkeys flinging themselves from tree branches, jumping around, and chattering nonstop. He meant that our minds were in constant motion. The mind is full of thoughts like dozens of monkeys, all clamouring for attention. Some monkeys induce fear, some of them are stress-causing and some of them are really naughty. Some of them are well-behaved too.

Intrigued, I thought about this idea further. I then read up extensively on the topic. The more I read, the more I understood. It seemed like that the key to solving many of the problems I was hearing about lay in understanding this concept better. I decided to categorise these monkeys into four types. I tried to get under their skin and get to the root cause of the suffering they bring about. Eventually, I had enough material and ideas for an entire book.

This book is the result of what I gathered from my interactions with thousands of young people and my understanding of their issues. Through these interactions I understood how their minds work, what stops them, what pushes them, what makes some of them winners, and how some of them lose sight of their big dreams.

This book is intended to help these young people dive into the inner core of their puzzled minds, now, not later when it's too late, and scoop out what's best for them.

*Think and Win like Dhoni* helped people in *knowing* what is important. This book will help you in *implementing* it.

Read it with an open mind and find out all about the monkeys that are an integral part of our lives.

*Now, let us get to know these monkeys a little better. Though they live with us, most of us don't know our own roommates.*

# Meet the Monkeys

Think back about your last twenty-four hours.

Did a peculiar loud voice tell you to do something 'Tomorrow'?

Did you hear voices that said: 'Don't do that!', 'This will break you!' and 'That's too scary!'

Did you make a decision only to change it two minutes later? Did you experience mood swings and your emotions switching rapidly from happy to gloomy, in control of yourself to feeling powerless and so on?

Did you manage to say no to that very tempting piece of junk food and motivate yourself to exercise instead?

All of these instances, both good and bad, are your monkeys at work.

These monkeys are your roommates! Knowing them is a step towards knowing 'you' better and bringing out the best in yourself.

The monkey that was telling you to put things off to tomorrow was the Procrastinator Monkey, the P-Monkey for short. He could well be labelled the Lazy Monkey. We will meet him in a while. But I am sure you will recognise him. If you have looked at your face in the mirror lately and spotted signs of that double chin growing … yes, yes … that's probably his 'achievement'.

That voice of alarm that warned you about danger and got you all worked up came from the family of the Fear Monkey.

When you couldn't make up your mind and quickly moved from being angry to being sad, from dull to super-excited and so on and never figured out why this was happening and why you were behaving the way you behaved … just like a drunk person, that was the Drunk Monkey at work!

There were also times when a calm voice told you to do the right thing and it felt good. This came from your very own Human Monkey, the monkey that always wants the best for you. This monkey is actually the good human in you. And his entire life is spent in keeping the other three and their families at bay.

Read on, I will introduce you to them real quick.

Let's meet them individually, before the P-Monkey tells you to drop the book and do something exciting on the internet.

Let's start with the P-Monkey itself!

### The P-Monkey

**Loves:** Gossiping
**Hates:** Discipline
**Lives:** In the grey zone of underperformance

- Have you delayed calling your best friend for days on end for no reason whatsoever?

- Have you observed yourself delaying payment on that pending telephone bill?
- Have you caught yourself staring at the dust gathering on the fan for weeks and not doing anything about it?
- Have you kept postponing an important task that has been occupying your mental space?

Let me tell you, it was not you who did it, it was a monkey inside you—the Procrastinator Monkey or the P-Monkey.

The P-Monkey will always prove to you with impeccable logic why it is not a good idea to execute something immediately. It will never let you execute NOW. This monkey loves tomorrows!

Tomorrow is the best day in the world view of this monkey. He will throw plenty of reasons at you to show you why tomorrow is the ideal time!

If you feel like you should quit smoking, this monkey will tell you to do it, but … tomorrow!

If you feel like you should get up and dispose of the garbage, this monkey will tell you to do it … tomorrow!

If you feel like saving money and cutting down on unnecessary expenses starting today, this monkey will tell you to start … tomorrow!

Because of this monkey, getting up becomes harder every morning, it takes three days to throw away that rotting apple and you happily pass by that object lying on the floor for days together without picking it up and restoring it to its rightful place. For a week, he makes you use the last remnants of the shampoo bottle as soap. In short, he is the one responsible for making you 'lazy'.

He loves 'Tomorrow'. The following poem, probably penned by the P-Monkey himself, is his life philosophy!

*Tomorrow—I love Tomorrow!*
*Today and now is going, going, gone!*
*Tomorrow is when the 'new me' will be born.*
*Tomorrow! Tomorrow! Tomorrow!*

Read on. We will soon learn where he stays, what his home looks like, how he prepares his 'to-do' list and spoils your day and much more. We will also learn how the Eagle of Wisdom can help the Human Monkey trap the P-Monkey.

### The Drunk Monkey

**Loves:** Flexibility
**Hates:** Being controlled
**Lives:** Different places, depending upon its mood

This is the monkey with random thoughts. This monkey is very unpredictable, just like a drunk person. Have you felt confused sometimes? Have you felt overloaded with negative and positive emotions? Have you switched from one decision to another real quick?

Yesterday, you bought a new potted plant for your balcony and you liked it. Today morning, you feel like the one you had rejected was better!

Have you sometimes felt life would be simpler if you

organised your things better? Maybe have a clean workspace or a clean room, for instance? Having decided that, you clean up your room or workspace and feel terrific. Everything is in place. You don't have to hunt for things and find everything quickly.

You then say to yourself, 'Wow, cleanliness is bliss! I will keep my room super-clean, my socks in place and my towel where it should be!'

It all goes well for two days and then you are back to square one. Yes, that's the Drunk Monkey for you. It doesn't operate based on logic. It's illogical and what's more, this monkey keeps changing colours.

**The Fear Monkey**

**Loves:** Protection
**Hates:** Experience of Change
**Lives:** In the Land of Terror

This monkey is always protective and avoids change. He is especially loud in setting off an alarm instantly, pointing out to all the things we should worry about and everything that could go wrong. Typically, this monkey is bound to make such utterances:

*'Remember the last time …? Your face was red! With shame and despair and failure and pain! Don't forget, I say, don't ever forget!'*

*'No, no … don't say that … they might make fun of you. What will they think? You might sound dumb!'*

*'They will never let you take the big steps. Don't be ambitious.'*

On the good side, this monkey is only trying to protect you. But by keeping you in a constant state of fear, he also curtails your ability to take risks. The Fear Monkey often affects your confidence.

Till the time the Human Monkey is able to deal with each one of these monkeys and exercise some degree of control over them, life is not so complicated. But when they come together, it's impossible for the Human Monkey to remain in control.

### The Human Monkey

This is the monkey that wants all the good things for self, family and society. This monkey is actually YOU. It is your better judgement, which can analyse things and can think straight. It is you performing to the best of your abilities.

The guiding statement of this monkey is, 'Let's get to the TOP!'

**Loves:** Achievements
**Hates:** Excuses
**Lives:** In a state of tension constantly adjusting with the other monkeys

This monkey actually wants to be a high-achieving go-getter. He wants to be the best version of himself in everything. What he wants from life depends on his thinking. There are a few people for whom success is top priority, a few who accord the highest priority to relationships and there are others who prioritise peace and happiness. Based on what the person wants, this monkey operates accordingly.

The Human Monkey faces stiff competition from the other three.

Human behaviour actually depends on the monkey that is most active at that point of time. For example, if a person is on his way to an interview and is too scared to recall anything at that moment, we can conclude that the Fear Monkey is dominant at that point of time. By the time the person reaches the interview, he is able to calm himself. This is on account of the situation being brought under control by the Human Monkey. Similarly, there may be times when the P-Monkey or the Drunk Monkey is active.

## Understanding the Monkeys Better

In a manner of speaking, all human beings have evolved from monkeys. In fact, in some ways, we could still claim to possess the mind of a monkey. This analogy sounds slightly humorous, but it is actually quite important. Research has proven that humans have around 50,000 separate thoughts each day. Many of them are around the same topic. And when we think of something repeatedly, it results in confusion, indecisiveness, procrastination, fear and anxiety.

In our troubled human world, 70 per cent of those 50,000 thoughts are about the fears and pressures of day-to-day life. Life often has this tendency to wear us down. Being frustrated with life is a normal state of being for many.

Thoughts like, 'What will happen if I lose my job? What will happen if my partner leaves me? What if this client doesn't pay on time? Will the audience make fun of me? What will happen when I retire? What if I lose money? What will they think about me?' are fears that constantly harass us. Often, these are made out to be much bigger than they actually are due to our constant harping on them. How infuriating, energy-consuming, exhausting it all becomes at some point! Really tiring, right?

Now, imagine each thought as a branch. Your attention is the monkey that keeps swinging from one thought-branch to the other. Your attention, that is, the monkey in your head, confuses you by swinging from branch to branch within a fraction of a second. It can quickly induce fear, anger, love, jealousy and bring your ego into any situation.

Because of how our thoughts keep jumping from branch to branch, a lot of our energy goes into fire-fighting. Quite literally, we are swinging from one thought-branch to another before settling on one. These thoughts of fear, insecurity, ego, and pride take a toll on the body, leading to chronic stress.

In *You Can Heal Your Life*, Louise Hay says that our thoughts are in fact responsible for many of our physical ailments. One way to cope with this is to understand that there is a difference between us and our thoughts. Seriously, you are not your thoughts. You are more, much, much more.

How then do we control our thoughts? Quite simply, by controlling our monkeys.

In this book, we will master just that. We will learn to train our Human Monkey to control the other three. Undoubtedly, the Human Monkey wants to achieve more. Stress out less. Love more. Criticise less. But the others don't let him get on with what he wishes to achieve. This book is about how the Human Monkey can make sure his goals are fulfilled.

## What This Book Will Do for You

Through this book, you will learn how to tame these monkeys. You will learn to recognise who has hijacked your confidence in that moment of self-doubt. If you are afraid to take that first step and do something new, who's stopping you? If you can't seem to decide on what to wear, which monkey is confusing you? After you read this book, you will have answers to all these questions and more.

I have devised some techniques to help you. I will teach you how to feed cherries to these monkeys. I will introduce you to the Eagle of Wisdom that can save the Human Monkey. You will understand how the Candle of Hope will help your surpass every problem on your way to where you want to be.

I will also take you to the Purple Island. On the Purple Island, bad monkeys are inoperative. That means you can do what YOU want to, rather than what the monkeys want. But how do you get there? Is it that easy? If yes, then everybody would have, right? Why is this island purple? All these questions will be answered.

I will also draw your attention to the Box of Guilt, which takes away your peace.

And lastly, I will reveal the encrypted message that the Human Monkey keeps seeing all around but doesn't quite understand.

The message: *'nay ady acn eb het alts yad!'*

Let's begin the journey!

This message is the gist of book. See if you can solve it. Otherwise wait and read on…

# The Rich Man's Wives

A few months ago, I was watching a documentary on the Buddha. It was about a tale that the Buddha had supposedly narrated to his students. I hope it offers you the same perspective that it gave me.

The story stresses the value of good emotions, good memories, good karma and good thought processes. It talks about how these are the only things that matter. Everything else is temporary. But the unfortunate truth is that what's most important is the most ignored too!

In ancient times, it was very common for men to have more than one wife. An old man, who had four wives, lay on his deathbed. Knowing he was going to die soon, he called his fourth wife, whom he loved very much, to his bedside. For many years, he had indulged this wife the most. He had got her the best jewellery, the most expensive clothes and had given her the best of everything. He loved her, she loved him and they were always together.

He called her and asked, 'I want you to accompany me after I die. Will you come with me?'

She replied, 'What?! What are you saying? I love you very much, but I can't come with you. I am sorry.'

His heart broke. He couldn't believe her words. He thought to himself: 'I gave her the best of everything, but she ditched me in the end!'

In grief and despair he sent word to his third wife. She was second in his affections and he had done a great deal for her too.

'I want you to accompany me after I die. Will you come with me?' he asked.

She replied, 'How can you expect that? I can't come along and in any case, I have decided that after you die, I … I am … going to marry someone else! Sorry!'

This shocked him again. He had given her considerable attention, had indulged her and yet here she was, betraying him in his hour of need.

Now, he sent word to his second wife and asked her the same question. He had shared all personal matters with her and she was very close to him. To his dismay, she too gave him a similar reply. She said she could come with him up to the cemetery, but not beyond.

Finally, the man's last hope was his first wife. He had always misbehaved with her, had never given her any importance, or valued her and hadn't done anything special for her. He had always taken her for granted. She had always been his last priority. He felt ashamed and guilty to even ask her to accompany him. But he did so anyway.

Guiltily, he asked her, 'I am almost dying and leaving this world. I don't want to go alone. Will you accompany me?'

She said, 'Of course, I will come with you, my dear. I will be there with you forever.'

Tears welled up in the old man's eyes. He couldn't believe how much she cared for him.

He said, 'My dear, I have always ignored you. You looked poor and miserable in front of the other three. I never realised that it was only you who loved me truly and selflessly. I wish I had taken more care of you.'

This beautiful analogy of the four wives was explained thus by Lord Buddha:

- Every person has four wives/husbands.
- The fourth wife symbolises our body and its cravings. We work on our body and its beauty and do almost everything to keep it beautiful, but it leaves us the moment we die!
- The third wife symbolises our material wealth (money, property, jewellery etc.), that will go to someone else after we die.
- The second wife symbolises our relationships that can't accompany us beyond the grave.
- The first wife symbolises our mind, deeds and actions. Always with us, but remains unnoticed. It is the most important one, but is ignored and something that one often realises only towards the end of one's life.

Now, the question that struck me was, 'If the mind is so important, why don't we spend time with it? Why don't we nourish and develop it?' Most of us find it really difficult to handle the mind. We find it difficult to handle our own emotions. Sometimes, our own emotions make our life miserable. I am sure this happens to all of us. The mind can be our best friend or our worst foe. A lot depends on how we handle it.

Here is an example. In the illustration below, the boy wants to study and focus on his work. But the monkeys keep chattering among themselves, causing him to lose focus.

Sometimes, he gets excited about the '60% OFF' SMS he's got. At other times, he is worried about being handsome enough and hence, jittery about confessing his love to his crush. At other times, he is worried about qualifying for the cricket team and every now and then, he is tempted to order pizza even though it goes against his fitness resolution.

This 'mental noise' does not allow him to perform at his best.

'Mental noise' is the constant chatter of the mind that never stops. It is the inner conversation or the inner monologue that is constant. It analyses everything about our life, circumstances, and the people we meet.

In the introduction, we spoke about the four monkeys we are going to deal with: the P-Monkey, the Drunk Monkey, the Fear Monkey and the Human Monkey. The P-Monkey, the Drunk Monkey and the Fear Monkey prevent us from working towards our goal by affecting us negatively. Further in this book, you will see how the P-Monkey finds an excuse for leisure while the Drunk Monkey pops up according to whatever cocktail he has just had. The Fear Monkey on his part raises our cortisol levels. These monkeys sometimes work alone and sometimes in tandem with each other. Amidst all this, the poor Human Monkey almost always loses the battle. Whether alone or together, they prove to be roadblocks.

Let us consider the following scenarios.

### Scenario I

Two years ago, I wanted to get up every morning and just go to the gym straightaway. But this constant conversation in my head almost made me lose the battle of waking up early.

**Human Monkey:** Sfurti, let's go to the gym!

**P- Monkey:** No, it's raining today! What if you get sick? No, it's better to exercise at home.

**Human Monkey:** Every day, you come up with some excuse or the other, Sfurti. Now it's time to go!

**P- Monkey:** Oh, it's too late now, it's already 7.45 a.m. and there will be traffic on the road. If you are late for work today, your boss will kill you. Tomorrow, you can get up early and go to the gym.

**Human Monkey:** Okay, let's at least exercise here at home then.

**P- Monkey:** But you like doing it with music and if you play music now, everyone will get disturbed!

**Human Monkey:** Then let's do yoga silently!

**P- Monkey:** Oh, yoga, that's too boring! You need some rush while exercising!

By this time, you are already late and you have to get to work quickly.

The P-Monkey wins.

**Desired result:** Exercise and weight loss.
**Actual result:** Sleep and weight gain.

Let me try and show you how these monkeys often work in tandem. Here is an example of how the monkeys work together to paralyse us.

## Scenario II

Karan wants to study as he knows it's important for him to finish his History syllabus quickly. Observe how all the monkeys inside Karan's head interact.

**Human Monkey:** We will focus on our work for next two hours.

**P-Monkey:** Pooja must have posted last night's party pictures on Instagram. Why don't you just check it out and get back to your studies? After all, it'll only take a minute!

**Human Monkey:** No, we did the same thing last time and got lost in the deadly world of social media.

**Drunk Monkey:** Go, check it out. Just promise yourself that you will get back to studying in exactly one minute.

After checking the post:

**Drunk Monkey:** Why has Nihar commented on this picture … that means he must like her … what if they start dating, what will you do?

**Fear Monkey:** Quick, just call her and take her out a movie today!

And in the end, Karan loses focus, and despite wanting to study, he doesn't.

The wild monkeys win.

**Desired result:** Finish studying History.

**Actual result:** Going for a movie. No significant progress in studies.

### Scenario III

Alex wants to finish a critical work assignment before the deadline. He is tired but knows that the assignment is critical. Late in the night, after returning home from a hard day's work, he is seated at the table in his bedroom.

**After ten minutes:**
Something inside his head says, 'You are tired. Why don't you sit on the bed and work?'

**After another ten minutes:**
'Why don't you put a pillow behind your head to give it more support?'

**Another ten minutes:**
'Sit comfortably. Stretch your legs.'

**Another ten minutes:**
'It's getting cold ... go get a blanket.'

Ten minutes later, Alex gently slides into the blanket. The presentations and reports are undone on the laptop. The laptop slips into sleep mode while Alex moves onto dreamland.

**After six hours:**
'Oh My God! I wanted to finish these reports last night. Why the hell did I sleep? I am such a useless person!'

Sounds familiar?

How many of us decide to do something and then don't do it? This leads to precipitation of guilt. This thick layer of guilt leads to lack of self-belief. To put it simply, the person stops believing that he is worth something. Before getting into the book, there is something you need to know: what is stored in your Box of Guilt.

A lot of people want to do several things in their lives but not all of them are able to. The reason is their inability to control their minds. In my first book, *Think and Win Like*

*Dhoni*, I talked about how it was Dhoni's mind and his ability to control it that made all the difference. But how many of us can actually do that? It is easy to say but difficult to implement. Find out why!

Now, let's take a peek into the Box of Guilt!

> **Box of Guilt:** A box full of all the regrets and unwanted activities that you really want to avoid.

Look at the questions below and answer them truthfully.

1. Why didn't I exercise today?
2. Why didn't I study?
3. Why am I spending so much time on YouTube?
4. Why am I spending so much money, why can't I save?
5. Why am I eating junk food?
6. Why didn't I handle the situation peacefully?

For many people, these might appear to be simple questions. For many others, these questions could be troublesome. Their Box of Guilt is a big, big one with plenty of regrets stored in it, some of them very fundamental.

**Reality Check:** What is in your Box of Guilt?

During a motivational lecture, I requested members of the audience to write down all the things they thought they could have done but couldn't because of their own actions and inaction.

An engineer spoke of how he couldn't do well in his medical entrance exam because he was too indisciplined and lazy. He was forced to go into engineering thereafter and didn't like it. It seemed to me that the P-Monkey had curtailed his Human Monkey from doing its best.

Another person spoke of his temper issues and relationship problems. His behaviour was unpredictable and his mood swings often got the better of him. His Drunk Monkey appeared to be very active.

People came up with many such guilts. Obviously, we cannot wallow in guilt forever. But the first step to getting rid of it is to realise which monkey was the culprit. This will give us a better understanding and set us free from this guilt!

The past is of course, irredeemable. But, our future lies ahead of us. Gearing up to beat our monkeys by making it a point to stick to our schedules, following a super-disciplined routine and remaining focused on our goals to achieve the maximum is critical.

### Introspection Time

Let's start afresh. Let's write down everything that make us feel guilty or inferior sometimes. Having done that, identify which monkey was responsible for ruining things in the past. (Example: not clearing an entrance exam, not being a great public speaker, unstable mind/indecisive nature, lack of confidence, arguing with colleagues at work and so on.)

1. ______________________________
2. ______________________________
3. ______________________________
4. ______________________________

These were the 'achievements' of our monkeys.

Now, let's list down the things that we actually want to achieve! What results do we want? Together, we will make sure our monkeys don't ruin things this time around.

1. ______________________________
2. ______________________________
3. ______________________________
4. ______________________________
5. ______________________________

Once you have finished, let's get down to knowing our monkeys better and in that process, know ourselves better!

### Points to Remember

- The human mind is full of monkeys. They are the reason for your sudden mood swings.
- The Fear Monkey constantly reminds you of all the things that could go wrong.
- The Drunk Monkey exhibits unpredictable behaviour.
- The P-Monkey tells you why it is not a good idea to do this job right now.
- The Human Monkey attempts to move ahead inspite of distractions from the other monkeys.
- Thoughts trouble the human mind and are often the main source of disease in the human body.
- It is important to understand these monkeys to move ahead and deal with them smartly.

# The P-Monkey or the Lazy Monkey

The P-Monkey (the Procrastinator Monkey) is a tough nut to crack. You probably don't even sometimes realise that he is working hard to make you do things that he wants you to do.

It's because of the P-Monkey that your social media handles are so vibrant! When overdone, these things waste your time. He knows that. You know that. But, hey, it is so much fun and therefore, you should turn over a new leaf … tomorrow! The P-Monkey is ready for fun instantly, but loves to do everything else tomorrow.

He wants to be a better person, but tomorrow!

Think of all the times you have underperformed because you weren't prepared enough. Think of all the useless shopping you have done. Look at your wardrobe and check out all the unnecessary clothes you bought. Think of the time you were a couch potato and spent hours lounging in front of the TV. You did all of this to get away from doing something else that was more important. Well, all of that was the P-Monkey at work.

What is the actual definition of procrastination?

Procrastination: the act of ruining your own life for stupid, demeaning reasons like:

- Let me take a small nap.
- Let me watch the next episode of *Game of Thrones*.
- Let me finish the next level of Candy Crush.
- Let me wonder about who is dating whom.
- Let me ponder about why she is thirty-two, but still not married.
- ______________________________
- ______________________________

Feel free to add to this list.

We all want to achieve something, we all desire something bigger, better and more significant. We all want that great body, those admirable work ethics, to work for that well-known company and that envious lifestyle. We all want to achieve world-class results.

Pop psychology writer Malcolm Gladwell says that deliberate 10,000 hours of practice is needed to become world-class in any field. But leave alone 10,000 … the truth is that most of us can't even focus for three hours at a stretch. Forget about three hours, I see many people struggling to focus even for an hour!

It all boils down to this question: Why can't we do what we actually want to do?

The simple answer is procrastination. A simple and succinct word.

And the solution to those who want to move ahead in life is just as simple.

Here's a simple exercise for you to try out now!

**Step 1:** Go back to what you did yesterday.
**Step 2:** Think about whether you were really productive.

If yes, that's great!

If no, who or what stopped you? What were the things you should have absolutely avoided?

All those things that you think could have been avoided are courtesy the P-Monkey. He was the one throwing all the useless distractions your way to make his life simple.

Procrastination has been a challenge that humans have faced since ancient times. Struggling, delaying, avoiding and offering excuses on issues that matter is an old habit. The problem is so timeless that ancient Greek philosophers had coined a word to describe this behaviour. They called it 'akrasia' which essentially means, the state of acting against your better judgement. Yes, your better judgement actually gets paralysed when your P-Monkey traps you.

But no, it's not your fault. We have never been given the correct tools to understand and fight this state. We've only heard our parents say, 'Please be disciplined. If you destroy time today, time will destroy you someday!' They never bothered to tell us how.

Now here we are:

- We need to make sure that people with deadlines avoid checking social media notifications frequently.

- We need to figure out how people interested in losing weight avoid taking those naps as excuses to not exercise.
- Students who need to be studying should avoid making those fancy boomerangs.
- ____________________________________________
- ____________________________________________

Feel free to add to this list.

How indeed?

Instead of merely telling us (the victims of this state) that fancy quote about discipline, perhaps our parents should have explained to us why we were behaving in a certain way, and what the way out of it was. How does one get over the tendency to keep on postponing things?

Nobody explained to you why your mind doesn't allow you to go to the gym!

Nobody explained to you why you are the last person to hand in your submissions!

Nobody explained to you why your mind moves in the exact opposite direction of where you actually want it to!

Sadly, neither have we attempted to understand our own behaviour.

To state things simply, it is the P-Monkey who is responsible for this. For super-disciplined people, this monkey is in an almost-dormant state, but for those who are struggling to find their towel every day, this monkey is in the active state.

The Human Monkey wants everything that is good for you. He is that voice in your head that says, 'This is the ideal time to do this project. Let's do it!'

The P-Monkey will give you ideas like, 'Let's go on YouTube first and do some research.' Once on YouTube, you are likely to spot the promo of a new movie, the video of a new song ... and soon, you are elsewhere! Time is wasted, work does not get done and frustration crops up.

For most people, the Human Monkey is the frustrated soul that doesn't understand why he is doing all this. He blames himself! This blame keeps filling up the Box of Guilt.

In the scenario detailed below, the Human Monkey wants to go for a root canal treatment. Observe how the P-Monkey stops him.

**Human Monkey:** Let's go for that dental treatment. Let's act right away before it comes to a point where we have to replace the entire tooth, which will cost a bomb.

**P-Monkey:** Hmm ... go on Saturday.

**Human Monkey:** Okay, fine.

**Saturday is soon here:**

**Human Monkey:** Let's go.

**P-Monkey:** Aren't you feeling a little sick today? And the dental treatment will be painful. Let me get well. The tooth decay is just about beginning. It is not an urgent situation.

The Human Monkey kept prodding you to go, but the P-Monkey kept throwing up excuses, one after the other.

**A few days later:**

**Human Monkey:** The tooth has started to hurt badly. Let's go today!

**P-Monkey:** Stop by after office since it is on the way.

**After arriving at the dentist's:**

**P-Monkey:** Oh no, there is long queue!
**Human Monkey:** Let's wait.
**P-Monkey:** You have lot of pending work, the pain is very basic, book an appointment and come again.

This is how the P-Monkey will keep on delaying things, often by giving you a sense of false security.

In most situations, the P-Monkey prevents us from doing anything constructive till the Human Monkey gets aggressive, gets into his Power Zone and demands that action be taken immediately!

**Consider a few more instances:**

**Human Monkey:** My weight has gone up by three kilos. It's time to hit the gym.
**P-Monkey:** Nope, don't worry, nothing will happen. You are looking good, chubby-chubby, and you are not fat. Just look at Mrs Sharma.

**Another instance:**

**Human Monkey:** I have time today, let me start working on my new book.
**P-Monkey:** Okay. A quick e-mail check and then, you can begin.

Once online, the P-Monkey gets excited and starts doing something else that was not on the agenda.

**P-Monkey:** Let's read something about the deadly Blue Whale Challenge. Also, by the way, check out Amazon reviews on that new gadget you have been wanting to buy.

Soon, before you know it, you are checking out the discounted price of the latest iPhone on Amazon.

Now, it's already 4.30 p.m. and you have to rush for your next appointment.

This is how the P-Monkey acts like a slow poison, and hour after hour, day after day, week after week, kills time, frustrating the Human Monkey.

In an ideal scenario, the P-Monkey must not be allowed to get active at all. But it is the most active among those who seem to be looking for external reasons for things that did not work out. Like that lost opportunity for a promotion or those 'few' extra kilos that seem to have appeared out of nowhere.

The P-Monkey enjoys leisure. He thinks, what's the point of sweating in the gym, if I can play Candy Crush in an air-conditioned room and relax? What's the point of disturbing my early morning sleep for yoga? Why should I avoid ice cream when it is so tasty? Why solve those difficult maths problems when there is a new Kylie Jenner post on Instagram?

For the P-Monkey, the Human Monkey is an old fellow who is bent on making its life difficult.

Do you put your diet off by a 'few hours' when you see something you want to eat? Do you make exceptions to your exercise routine on a 'cold' day? Are you always choosing the 'easy' option in situations? If your answer to all these questions is yes, then your P-Monkey is pretty active.

The P-Monkey wants to navigate your boat according to his convenience. But since he is an unqualified navigator, you are unable to understand the direction in which your life is headed. The P-Monkey never considers past experiences or future ambitions. He just wants to play games on the chessboard in front of him at that moment, which unfortunately will yield nothing major and significant.

I have seen many people say that they hate themselves. They have suffered a great deal in life because of their 'let's do it tomorrow' attitude. They lose confidence and self-respect and start to believe that they are good at nothing. Even if they start doing something new with lots of hope and positivity, their determination goes out of the window midway because of the interference of the P-Monkey.

List out the things you have lost because of the P-Monkey.

Why am I asking you to do this? No, not to make you feel terrible! This is just a realisation tool which will help you counterattack his excuses!

1. ______________________________
2. ______________________________
3. ______________________________
4. ______________________________
5. ______________________________

## The Palace of the P-Monkey

Once, the Human Monkey was frustrated because he couldn't clear an entrance exam. He could clearly see that it was because of his indiscipline and laziness, meaning, the P-Monkey was in action. The Human Monkey resolved to make sure that the P-Monkey didn't waste time or cause his schedule to go haywire henceforth.

The next day, the Human Monkey started his day early, put the phone away while working, prepared a timetable, started early every day and got down to work! This went on for three days … and then the P-Monkey returned!

Has this happened to you? You were very consistent for the first few days of your diet or gym or study schedule but a few days later, you began to lose focus.

Similarly, after a few days, the Human Monkey realised that it was almost impossible to get rid of the P-Monkey so easily.

'I need to find a way. I need to learn the tools to fool him!' the Human Monkey told himself.

It was time to catch, confront and do away with the P-Monkey forever, thought the Human Monkey. It was time to pay the P-Monkey a visit at his palace.

The reason I am calling it a palace is because the P-Monkey actually lives like a king! His palace is a palatial one. It will take your breath away. It has beautifully painted walls, tinted rainbow-coloured window panes, a well-manicured garden and a majestic door.

The tastefully done interiors and the antique furniture will leave you spellbound. The home is equipped with the latest

technologies. The P-Monkey makes sure he is well-supplied with all the gadgets necessary for luxury and comfort. He likes to spend a lot of his money on big cars, mobile phones, video games, house interiors and so on.

When the Human Monkey visited the palace, there were gadgets all over the place, many of them fairly new. The huge TV in the living hall was airing the latest movie. There was plenty of popcorn. The sofa was soft and comfortable. And yet, there was plenty that was wrong.

It was stinking so much that the Human Monkey desperately wanted to get out and breathe some fresh air. One sock from a pair lay in the kitchen and the other was lying near the TV remote. There were chocolate wrappers below the bed ... and the room smelt foul because of the left-over pizza from three days ago! The rooms were really messy and poorly maintained.

The P-Monkey loves living in beautiful, lavish places, but keeps them messy, and cluttered. He is too lazy to maintain them. He would love to stay in clean places too ... provided someone else was doing the cleaning!

He bought plenty of gadgets but soon got bored of them. If there was a new gadget in town, the P-Monkey had to have it but couldn't be bothered about doing away with the old ones.

Everywhere the Human Monkey looked—on the walls, cabinets and elsewhere—'tomorrow' was etched in big, bold letters.

The Human Monkey then discovered the P-Monkey's to-do list:

- Clearing up iPhone data while writing an assignment.
- Checking the cost of those Nike shoes on Flipkart.
- Refreshing Facebook feed repeatedly to check out what's new and looking at photographs till you find pictures of your friend with her boyfriend.
- Daydreaming about 'how I will become the Prime Minister of the country'.
- Thinking about the latest dress of a famous celebrity.
- Looking at the latest pictures and getting confused about which one should go up on social media.
- Thinking about your ex and wondering what she must be thinking.
- Touching that new pimple hundred times a day!

As is obvious, each one of the above tasks is unproductive and could have been used for something else resulting in concrete achievements.

Clearing up iPhone data while writing an assignment.

Checking the cost of those Nike shoes on Flipkart.

Refreshing Facebook feed repeatedly to check out what's new and looking at photographs till the time you find picture of your friend with her boyfriend.

Daydreaming about 'how I will become the Prime Minister of the country'.

Thinking about the latest picture of Kylie Jenner.

Looking at your latest pictures and getting confused about which should go on social media.

Thinking about your ex- and wondering what he or she must be thinking.

Touching that new pimple hundred times a day!

In another spot in the house, the Human Monkey discovered the 'achievement' list of the P-Monkey!

1. Increased body weight by ten kilos.
2. Made 1000 Facebook friends and got 3423 Instagram followers.
3. Crossed the 73th level of Candy Crush.
4. Successfully fought with the snooze button on the alarm and got up exactly fifteen minutes before school.
5. Kept you short by five per cent each semester.
6. Shopped for the entire collection of Forever New.
7. Watched all the latest movies at PVR.
8. Attended all birthday parties.
9. Watched all videos forwarded on WhatsApp.
10. Checked all the new Hollywood gossip.

Even as the Human Monkey was trying to process all that he had seen in the palace of the P-Monkey, he remembered a recent incident.

One day, the Human Monkey was busy with a project and determined to finish it that day. Even as he pondered over the project, a little voice within spoke up, 'Isn't it time to take a break? You've been working for an hour.'

'Sssshh,' retorted the Human Monkey. 'I am going to finish my project! Don't disturb!'

'Okay, I won't ... but I still think, tomorrow is a Monday and Monday is the best day to work. Sunday is a day for rest!'

The P-Monkey was up to his tricks.

'Listen,' said the P-Monkey in a soft voice. 'Clearly, you are tired. Tomorrow, start afresh. You might end doing poor quality work if you continue doing it today. Better take a break.'

'No, I can't do that. I MUST finish the project today,' the Human Monkey replied.

The P-Monkey spoke up again, 'I don't understand why you are like this. Life is beautiful. Why do you have to work so much? Your father has earned enough. You can sit, relax and enjoy, can't you, buddy?'

'I need to perform well. My family expects a lot from me. It's time for me to be focused and consistent. But because of you, I can't perform. So please stop making these stupid excuses. Please let me stay away from the phone. Please let me finish.'

'Tomorrow ... tomorrow ... tomorrow is the best time my dear ... how can you stay away from the phone today, sweetheart? After all, that's my favourite food. The phone is my favourite snack, gossip is my favourite dinner and shopping is my favourite pastime!'

'I'm requesting you politely. Stop wasting my time.'

'Honey, you don't understand .... I need the phone, gossip and shopping to keep me fit. Else I will get sick, I will lose weight. Oh! Now go ahead, it's time to eat some wafers and then take a nap. Move it. Work can wait!'

'Polite conversation won't work with you. Why are you like this?

I earn. ———→ You spend.
I diet. ———→ You eat junk.
I save time. ———→ You waste time.
I exercise. ———→ You sleep.

I am going to kill you one day!'

The Human Monkey started to fight with the P-Monkey. But the P-Monkey was huge and powerful and was only injured. The P-Monkey walked away, down, but not out.

Having incapacitated the P-Monkey, even if for a while, the Human Monkey was able to focus. He woke up on time, exercised each morning, ate healthy food and began to feel energetic and happy. This discipline lasted for all of three days.

The P-Monkey had returned!

**P-Monkey:** Oh, it's Sunday. Let me sleep for fifteen minutes more.

And an hour passed by.

**Human Monkey:** Oh my God, it's 8.15, Dad is coming today. I need to rush to the airport to pick him up. Gosh, how could I sleep so much!

The exercise routine for that day was missed.

The pattern had been broken.

Exercising stopped, slacking began.

Healthy eating stopped, binging on junk began.

Saving stopped, spending began.

Studying stopped, YouTubeing began!

The Human Monkey soon grew tired of his poor results and poor habits. Day after day, his resolve kept slipping. The P-Monkey offered such tough competition that the Human Monkey could not handle it. The feeling worsened each passing day and the Human Monkey began to hate himself. Much as he wanted to come out of the situation, he just could not find a long-lasting solution.

The Human Monkey was stressed, depressed, shattered and lonely. Parents and teachers humiliated the Human Monkey for his poor performance but he was not able to figure a way out. On one such depressing day, the Human Monkey sat alone in the park thinking about the scolding he had received from teachers for not having completed assignments on time. He cried out in pain, 'God, what should I do? In spite of having the desire to perform well, I am not able to! I think I am just useless! I can't do anything good! I really want to quit, I can't seem to perform and I am just so bad at everything! Show me the way, God, to beat my laziness.'

There was no voice from the skies. Only silence.

This is not an unusual story. How many times has it happened to you?

You decided on something, did it for few days or weeks and then things slipped and you could not make things whole again. Can you think of all the possible resolutions you made? Just imagine where you would have been today if those resolutions had actually stayed with you.

Visiting the palace of the P-Monkey had reminded the Human Monkey about everything that was wrong. But he still didn't know how to set things right. Was there no hope at all?

## The Eagle of Wisdom

The Eagle of Wisdom had been watching the Human Monkey the whole time. The pain, frustration, desire to perform, dissatisfaction due to under performance, everything. Soon enough, the Human Monkey was at the park again crying for help. The Eagle of Wisdom finally decided to show up.

The Eagle of Wisdom is mighty in size and majestic in disposition. His feathers are preened to perfection. The aristocratic air about the way the eagle flapped his wings was like a warning to the other petty creatures about not to mess with him. He is kind and composed, poignant and dignified and has an easy air around him even as he appears totally in command. His eyes are wise yet soft. There is an air of assurance he carries with ease. He is known for his alertness, sharp observations and knowledge.

He sat beside the Human Monkey and introduced himself.

'Hi, I am the Eagle of Wisdom. I heard you crying from a distance. What's the matter?'

The poor Human Monkey started to tell him the whole story. The eagle listened quietly. Once he sensed that the story had been completed, he offered the wisdom that he had gathered over the years.

'I have seen people spoiling their careers, their relationships and their health because of procrastination. Performers underperform! The capable lose! The deserving lose out!

'I don't want you to be yet another victim. You are very keen to change and improve. I have been observing you for the past many days and that's why I thought I'd help you out. To deal with the P-Monkey, you need to be really patient and consistent.

'The P-Monkey loves to keep you in the Grey Zone of Underperformance. In this zone, a person's oxygen is self-hatred and carbon dioxide is guilt,' said the Eagle of Wisdom.

'What is the Grey Zone of Underperformance?' asked the Human Monkey.

'It is a land where the entire community of procrastinators live. The soldiers here want to take over your mind and hence keep manipulating you. There are only two types of people they can't handle and they are only afraid of courageous people. Before I tell you more about this, tell me, why do you give the P-Monkey the opportunity to attack you?' replied the Eagle.

'How am I giving the P-Monkey an opportunity? And what are the two types of people that he can't handle?' asked the confused Human Monkey.

'Look at your dirty socks. Clearly, cleanliness is not your strength. The P-Monkey finds it really tough to be with ultra-clean people. People who keep their wardrobes in order, their beds made and their tables clean, tend to be in control of themselves. The P-Monkey can't handle these kind of people. This is the first type. He loves to be with unhygienic and indisciplined people.

'First, clear the mess at home and then I will help you compete with him and defeat his entire army. Let's meet tomorrow at 8 a.m. Don't forget to bring your schedule of the last three days.'

The Human Monkey felt really happy. His goal appeared closer now. At home, the Human Monkey cleaned up his room, organised his wardrobe, washed his dirty clothes and socks and felt at peace. The next morning, he got up early, dedicated time to exercise and got ready to meet the Eagle. But he was delayed by ten seconds.

The Human Monkey was quite excited to tell the Eagle of Wisdom everything. But before he could, the Eagle asked, 'Why are you late? The fact that you don't value your ten seconds is a clear message to your P-Monkey that he can waste all the time if wants. You need to understand that you can't beat him unless you start improving on small things. For instance, your bag still looks quite messy. Clean it up. Start cleaning up all of the small things. This really irritates him. When you wake up, make your bed immediately. It's early in the day and the P-Monkey can't attack that early.'

The Eagle of Wisdom then gave the Human Monkey a list:

- Read 15 minutes before sleeping!
- Make a To-Do list and keep it in your pocket everyday!
- Set 40 minute targets and allow yourself a 2 minute break, but make sure the P-Monkey doesn't fool you in those 2 minutes. If he tries to attack, tell yourself, it's a trap! TRAP! TRAP! TRAP!
- Clean your room every day or every alternate day.
- Remember to consume three to four litres of water a day to keep your energy levels up!
- Don't touch your phone 10000 times in an hour!
- Don't quickly gravitate to the new notification when you get on the phone. Finish your task and check the notification.
- Try to cut down on junk food!
- Never leave things for tomorrow. Remember the P-Monkey loves tomorrows!

The Eagle continued, 'These are very simple things in life which give a very loud and clear message to the P-Monkey that discipline is your highest priority. Follow this for a week and I will teach you a few tricks to enter the Colour Zone of Performance.'

The Human Monkey kept to a strict schedule for a week and began to feel the difference. But throughout he was worried and scared that the P-Monkey would return.

Regardless, he made sure he followed whatever he had learnt and was excited about being introduced to the Colour Zone of Performance.

In between, the P-Monkey did try to make a comeback. But this time, the Human Monkey was a lot smarter and could handle that! Whenever the P-Monkey tried to attack, the Human Monkey pulled out the to-do list and began executing the next task on the list. And the P-Monkey beat a hasty retreat.

After two weeks, the Human Monkey and the Eagle of Wisdom met again at the same spot.

'So, did you follow all that was asked of you?' asked the Eagle.

'Yes,' the Human Monkey replied.

'How are you feeling now?' asked the Eagle.

'I feel in control. I think I can set any goal and plan on how to reach it. I have started to believe in myself,' said the happy Human Monkey.

'So that's the Colour Zone of Performance for you. This is where you should try to stay the most. The Colour Zone of Performance is the area where you will be dominant! You will be the driver!

'This zone is called the Colour Zone because of its freshness, richness and liveliness. Those who spend most of their time in this zone can produce extraordinary results and develop amazing relationships.

'In the Colour Zone, the air is filled with self-confidence. The land is fertile enough to convert the mediocre into the strong. The clouds are made up of achievements. And the water is filled with clarity.

'On the other hand, in the Grey Zone, the air is filled with anxiety. The land is infertile and life is a struggle. The clouds are made up of guilt. And the water is filled with muddy goals.

'High performers spend most of their time in the Colour Zone and are witness to the fruit of their efforts. They energise themselves by taking ample breaks but are in full control of their P-Monkey. A peak performer knows how to tame the P-Monkey. Whenever the P-Monkey seeks leisure, they know how to handle him.

'Who likes to practise the same dialogue a hundred times a day? Not many. But that's exactly what successful actors do! Who likes to practice a single stroke a hundred times a day? But, that's what successful cricketers do! Who likes to solve the same math problem again and again? But, that's what successful IITians do!

'They know how to control their P-Monkey. They know how to make the monkey work for them rather than make themselves slaves to the monkey.

'Life is really short. If you are twenty-five today, then, considering that the average life span of human beings is about seventy years, you only have around 16,425 days left.

'Do you want to spend the rest of your life just roller-coastering on your Facebook feed or in taking that perfect selfie?

'No, life has a purpose. Life has to have a meaning. Procrastination not only kills your time, but also kills your best performance.

'What's the second category of people that the P-Monkey cannot deal with?' asked the Human Monkey in curiosity.

'The second category of people are people with vision. People who can see the influence of the present on their future. People who can connect their present selves to their future selves. You should understand how this present hustle will secure your future or how this present comfort will make your future insecure!

'So, let's look at some actual ways that will help tame the monkey. Let's learn the process of transition from the Grey Zone to the Colour Zone. To begin with, focus on cleanliness and learn to value time.'

Soon, the Human Monkey started to see some great results in life. He was able to allocate time to studies, presentation skills, communication skills and writing and even to social media. He kept track of time and reduced wastage of time.

## Entering the Colour Zone of Performance

The next week, the Human Monkey met the Eagle of Wisdom again. This time he was focused and ready with a to-do list. The Eagle taught the Human Monkey the following tricks.

### 1. Ask for details

Exams were coming up in the next semester and the Human Monkey wanted to tame the P-Monkey before that. The Eagle of Wisdom taught him a few lessons. Let's see how the Human Monkey trapped the P-Monkey.

**Human Monkey:** Next year, we have to apply for the GRE!
**P- Monkey:** Oh ... yeah!
**Human Monkey:** So, we will study hard.

**P-Monkey:** Yes, you must start studying after the first of August, once your mid-semester exams are done.

**Human Monkey:** Hmm okay. But when?

**P-Monkey:** I told you. 1 August is the date.

**Human Monkey:** Should I pay the deposit fee of Rs 1000 to the library so that we can study there for three hours after college every day?

(Now the P-Monkey starts to feel the pressure!)

**P-Monkey:** Why the hell do you want to spend Rs 1000 to study? Why waste money?

(He wasn't actually bothered about wasting money, he just didn't want to study every day and get trapped.)

**Human Monkey:** How about you spending Rs 8000 on that stupid video game?

**P-Monkey:** Hmm … I regret that!

**Human Monkey:** So, from Monday the 1st, we will study in the library from 5.30 to 8.30 every evening. This schedule will continue for three months. Have a great time! Bye!

Trap it!

Commit to things such that you cannot back out. Every human being loves to relax. But it's all about how we can handle the internal battle between the urge to work and the urge to just remain in the comfort zone.

Here, the technique used was to commit to something since there was a possibility of procrastination. Just schedule it and declare it! Then you cannot back out. This is how you can enter the Colour Zone. This is how you can know and find your best self.

The P-Monkey loves planning for tomorrow. He loves daydreaming and hopes for everything to just happen. But when he plans, the P-Monkey makes vague noises. For example, if you want to learn Java, he will tell you, 'We will take up learning the language from January to March.' You will assume that this will definitely happen, but that is where you are fooled. You need to ask him for details. You need to block the dates. Under the influence of dedicated time and pressure, the P-Monkey loses his power.

So when this monkey tells you that he will get up and start exercising tomorrow, ask for a specific time. Better still, you decide the time. Tell him that you will hit the gym at 7.20 a.m. sharp. Else, the daydreaming and planning that do not take any effort will continue and it will always seem like you are on the verge of something without actually achieving anything.

**2. Burn the monkey's bridges**

Declare it in front of the world. The moment something is declared, the Fear Monkey makes sure that the P-Monkey starts work to save itself from public embarrassment. I wanted to write my first book and so I declared on Facebook that my first book on M.S. Dhoni would be out in the next six months. Now, by hook or crook, I had to do it. This is how burning bridges worked for me. This is how I didn't allow my P-Monkey to interfere.

Declare it!

Declare that you're going to lose weight. Declare that you're going to crack the GRE. Declare that you're going to do what you want to do! Have the guts, have the will.

Get … SET … GO!

### 3. Make your enemy list

What distracts you? Identify those factors. For example:

i. Facebook Whatsapp/Snapchat/Instagram notifications
ii. Worrying how you look in tagged pictures
iii. A new web series
iv. Assuming that you will turn over a new leaf 'tomorrow' and fooling yourself

Yes, make a list of things that distract you. And whenever you find yourselves doing these things … become aware and get back on track.

The moment you detect the presence of the P-Monkey and act against him, you will start working wonders.

Make a 'Stop Doing' list!

1. ______________________________
2. ______________________________
3. ______________________________
4. ______________________________
5. ______________________________

Now whenever you start doing any of these things, tell yourself it's the P-Monkey at work. Merely reminding yourself throughout the day can eliminate the presence of the P-Monkey.

**4. Oh … what am I doing?**

While studying, you sometimes find yourself getting lost in the deadly world of your cell phone. That's when you need to realise that this time was dedicated for studies or other important work. Ask yourself the question, 'Oh … what am I doing?' Your focus is likely to come back.

It can apply to eating habits as well. If you have decided to stay off junk food and friends compel you to indulge for just a bit, the P-Monkey starts to get excited. He is likely to prompt you to eat more. Ask yourself this question then.

**5. Reverse engineering**

Start becoming a person of vision. A person who can visualise their future. A person who sees the connection between their present and future selves.

Imagine your future self who is the result of procrastination and indiscipline. You definitely do not want to be that person. Remind yourself of the consequences of not finishing work on time. Imagine maintaining the same procrastinating attitude and ask yourself where you will be a year from today.

Whenever you find yourself losing focus, just think about your favourite celebrity or any other successful person and ask yourself, 'Is this the way champions are made?'

The most important thing is that you should realise the pain of procrastination. You should realise how damaging it is for you. You should realise what you will lose if you don't act in time.

I ask myself these questions often:

- What will I lose if I don't exercise every day?
- What will I lose if I don't stop eating junk food?
- What will I lose if I keep wasting my time on something useless?

**6. One more try! Can I do it now?**

Just imagine how things will be if you don't procrastinate for an entire year.

The next time you feel like you are tired and want to postpone that final push or feel you can't stretch for another mile, just calmly ask yourself, 'Can I try one more time?' This is how champions push themselves, this is how your work appetite grows and this is how you get into the habit of finishing, no matter what.

A day is exclusive. It never questions and never returns. How about making each day really productive? This will not only keep you away from garbage but will also satisfy your soul by taking you to the peak.

**7. 'He wants temporary pleasure and permanent pain.'**

Next time you fall back in love with your blanket even after the alarm rings, just tell yourself, 'The P-Monkey wants to give me temporary pleasure and permanent pain. Am I willing to pay the price?'

Let's just get up and do it!

**8. Just fool him!**

Tell him if you are allowed to work now, he will get the complete Sunday to watch his favourite *Game of Thrones*!

Just start getting rid of him at that moment! And start looking for the purple colour around you.

There is an island where this monkey loses his power: the Purple Island.

Read on. You will find it soon.

**Remember:**

1. We all want to win, but procrastination stops us.
2. Stop performing in the Grey Zone. You will not reach your peak potential.
3. The P-Monkey cannot deal with two kinds of people. Those who are disciplined and those with a vision.
4. Be organised. Start keeping a timer. This will help you realise how much time you waste.
5. Procrastination is a slow poison. Its effect is not immediate, but it is irreversible. Recognise when the P-Monkey is working on you. That mere realisation is enough to destroy the monkey's empire.
6. Make a Stop-Doing list.
7. Have patience. It takes time to change. But don't ever stop trying.
8. Consistency is key.
9. Keep looking for the purple colour around you (more on this later).

**Exercises for your Human Monkey**

Reflect: What does your Human Monkey actually want? And what does the naughty P-Monkey make you do?

| *Human Monkey WANTS* | *P-Monkey DOES* |
|---|---|
| | |
| | |
| | |
| | |
| | |
| | |
| | |

There is an island where this monkey loses his power: the Purple Island. We'll get there in the final chapter.

Read on.

# The Fear Monkey

Think back about your last few weeks. Have you, at any time in these past few weeks, felt a cold, clammy fear that prevented you from doing something you wanted to? Did it seem like some unseen force was pulling you back? Or whisper to you to desist from doing something since the consequences of failure, the voice reminded you repeatedly, were very high?

Maybe it was a public speaking assignment that you had boldly signed up for. Public speaking is considered the number one fear in the world. But, you decided to go ahead anyway. And a few days or maybe, even a few hours before you had to deliver, a voice in your head told you to drop out. It warned you of the consequences of doing a bad job. Your mind conjured up images of failure. You panicked. You were unsure. You cursed yourself for signing up.

And then, you backed out!

That was nothing but the Fear Monkey at work.

Whether it is a decision about appearing on stage or making an investment, the Fear Monkey loves to interfere by imagining the worst. A part of what this monkey does is to merely exercise natural caution. But, a part of this monkey is all about creating an irrational fear that paralyses.

Let's understand this monkey better with the help of a few scenarios.

**Scenario I**

I was always afraid of driving on highways. Every now and then, whenever I would consciously convince myself to get into the vehicle and just drive, a peculiar voice inside my head would always utter the word 'NO'.

**Human Monkey:** Sfurti, let's go for a drive!
**P-Monkey:** Do you have to go today? You've been so busy for the last few days. Why don't you just chill?

**Human Monkey:** You've been 'just chilling' all morning. You've had your rest. Why not do something now?

Even as I would be torn between 'just chilling' and 'doing something', a new character would then suddenly enter the conversation.

**Fear Monkey (suddenly making an appearance):** No, don't go … it's too frightening!
**Human Monkey:** Sfurti, take your vehicle and go to Mumbai.
**Fear Monkey:** No, it's too dangerous, look at the highway. What if you fall into a ditch and get lost in the lonely valley?
**Human Monkey:** When you will learn to drive on highways? Come on, take a chance and do it.
**Fear Monkey:** Why the hell do you want to drive, what will you learn from driving to Mumbai? Just imagine if you get hit by a bus … you will be bedridden for a month or you might die! Just take a cab.
**Human Monkey:** Sfurti, just go ahead. Don't be afraid!
**Fear Monkey:** A cab will be more comfortable as you will not have to drive. It's better to save your energy for something important. You can also work on the way.

Finally, the Fear Monkey would successfully convince me that it wasn't a good idea to drive, and win the argument. And the P-Monkey played its part by urging me to push the activity to a later date. The fears raised by the Fear Monkey actually prevented me from doing something that I could have.

**P-Monkey and Fear Monkey win.**

**Desired result:** Drive on the highway.
**Actual result:** Exactly the opposite.

How many of us have experienced this? There are these voices that constantly keep repeating something and stop us from doing something that is actually important.

For me it was driving. For you it could be something else, like volunteering to do some public speaking or taking a flight or going for a swim. These are activities that some people find difficult. To overcome their fear they have to try and force themselves to take that first step. They have to commit to at least making an attempt. But there is a voice within that keeps telling them that they shouldn't be taking it up.

### Scenario II

You are in an amusement park.

**Human Monkey:** Let's go and enjoy coming down from the highest slide. It's fun. Let us have a thrilling experience.

**Fear Monkey:** Are you mad? Have you gone out of your mind! We can't go there!

**Human Monkey:** But there are so many people doing just that. We are also wearing a thick jacket that will protect us.

**Fear Monkey (to himself):** Wait. Let me raise your anxiety level ... then you will automatically stay away from that slide!

### Scenario III

'I think I will use the stairs! I am in exercise mode. As it is, I am dieting too,' said Aashi.

'Hey, but it's on the eleventh floor and we are late,' said Adhiraj.

Now, Aashi's Fear Monkey spoke up, 'No, no, I can't enter that elevator. I am so scared. What if it stops in between? What if the controls fail and it stops and falls down?'

Exercise was just an excuse that Aashi was using … it was the Fear Monkey speaking for her because she did not want to take the elevator.

The Fear Monkey sometimes haunts our thoughts late in the night. While the Procrastinator Monkey's antics ruin your career and growth, the Fear Monkey can stress you out, almost to death.

The Fear Monkey is very demanding. He needs constant attention, like a newborn baby. He will beep like an alarm and constantly remind you about all the things that could go wrong. If you don't actively listen to him, he'll sneak in when you're sleeping, driving, having lunch, or when you are in the bathroom.

But here's the thing! He is never around when you are occupied. He only strikes when you are alone and aren't doing anything. I am sure that at least once in your lifetime you must have heard that self-destructive voice, that almost guarantees your loss before the actual competition begins. That is the Fear Monkey for you!

## THE FEAR MONKEY NEVER ATTACKS WHEN YOU ARE OCCUPIED!

Sometimes, the Fear Monkey comes in the form of a thought constantly going on at the back of your mind: 'What made you believe you could do this?'

Sometimes, it says: 'You will be broke!'

Sometimes, it forces you to think to yourself: 'What if it doesn't work?'

At other times, fear slowly seeps in when you're not paying attention. Have you noticed a peculiar feeling of dread that surfaces in your mind about an hour before you have to wake up? It is a kind of nightmare, isn't it? And then you wake up dreading the day ahead.

Then there are those quiet moments, when you are waiting in a long queue or waiting for your flight to take off. It is precisely at this time that the Fear Monkey strikes and asks you, 'What if your new product fails in the market? Are you aware of the stiff competition?'

And guess what, that one thought can ruin your day, as it is bound to trigger off a series of arguments and allegations going back and forth between the Fear Monkey and the Human Monkey.

Do you think you can then concentrate on the work at hand? Absolutely not! Many sportspeople, artists and singers have ruined their careers by just allowing the Fear Monkey to take control right when they are in the midst of a big day in their lives.

To a cricketer, the Fear Monkey may scream and say, 'This bowler has taken your wicket thrice. I don't think you can face him!'

To a singer, the Fear Monkey may scream and say, 'The entire world is watching, what if you lose your rhythm?'

To an author, the Fear Monkey may scream and say, 'This piece of writing is useless and nobody is going to publish it!'

Soon enough, the person starts to have doubts, his morale dips, his confidence is shattered and in extreme cases, he may even start to believe that he is useless.

The thoughts don't stop there. The Fear Monkey is constantly trying to trap you. He attempts to quicken your heartbeat, increase your blood pressure and make your nervous. And once you get nervous ... that is the tipping point! Nervousness is a sign of having surrendered to the Fear Monkey. Once you have, the Fear Monkey will make sure you stay with it in his cave and do not attempt to conquer newer horizons.

What cave? Read on to find out.

One of the odd things about the whole Fear Monkey syndrome is that it's quite a natural experience and seems quite personal. It's very difficult to share for fear of being made fun of.

Consider this example.

You are an entrepreneur and decide to attend an entrepreneurs' meet to meet like-minded people and understand how they go about their business. At the meet, you are interacting with people when all of a sudden, a fear creeps up on you. Now this time, it's not panic, it's doubt. It is a kind of internal monologue, much like this, 'Why have you have invested so much money on your office interiors? Who gave you the idea of using luxurious Italian marble? You have spent so much already.

'What if that client doesn't pay you on time?

↓

'What if your best employees start to leave you?

↓

'What if the office expenses do not get recovered?

↓

'You will be on the road! Your wife will leave you!

↓

'She will take your daughter with her!

All this doubting has just happened in under three seconds.

Yes ... it's hard to believe, but it happens!

If you are trying to call up your daughter and she isn't picking up her phone, within three seconds, the Fear Monkey starts to visualise the worst possible outcome.

If your boss calls you into his cabin, on your way there, you may begin to visualise yourself getting fired, not getting a new job, and even going bankrupt!

Sitting in the dentist's chair, you start to feel that the small needle is a bulldozer which will bore into your jaws and hurt you real bad.

Do you get such thoughts? Thoughts that are absolutely useless, waste your time and energy, weaken your will, and make you feel powerless?

Is your Human Monkey frustrated and fearful?

Let's make a list of things that the Fear Monkey keeps telling us. We will deal with each one of your fears! Remember, these are the triggers and we can only deal with the problem once we understand the problem.

1. ____________________
2. ____________________
3. ____________________
4. ____________________

Here's the story of a terrible memory lapse. James was once selected to speak at the annual event at his school. He was all prepared with his lines. Then suddenly, he was the victim of a cringe-worthy fifteen second blackout. He struggled to recall the name of the school's newly-appointed Vice-Principal. James' heart rate accelerated, his brain froze and his memory blacked out. In a speech addressed to the Vice-Principal himself, James forgot his name. He was the butt of all jokes at school for a week and felt extremely embarrassed. And this or something like this has happened to so many of us.

James was ousted from the school committee for humiliating the Vice-Principal. He couldn't make sense of the situation. He knew that the Fear Monkey tended to overpower him but he had attempted to keep the monkey away. But the monkey had come back anyway.

James and his Human Monkey were frustrated and why shouldn't they be?

The Human Monkey thought for a while and then began to question himself.

'From where did this fear of public speaking come? Why do others speak so confidently while I fumble? Why can't I express my ideas clearly? Why am I so afraid of rejection? Why am I such a loser? Why can't I fly freely in the sky, where I am worry-free, stress-free, and filled with pure peace and bliss?'

The Human Monkey in him realised that if he didn't kill the Fear Monkey, he would never achieve whatever he wanted to. After some days, the Human Monkey thought, 'Today, I am going to kill the fear inside me somehow.'

This is normal. Many of us resolve to become fearless going forward and the Human Monkey was no different. The Human Monkey decided to find the Fear Monkey and kill him. He decided to 'face its fears' once and for all. The Fear Monkey lives in the Land of Terror. Reaching there and confronting the Fear Monkey is not easy—it requires a lot of willpower and a brave heart.

This time too, the Human Monkey saw a sign board but with a different message.

**'yna yad nca eb eth salt ady!'**

Each time the Human Monkey saw this sign board, he felt a sense of renewed energy and started looking forward to life!

## Finding Your Way in the Land of Terror

The Land of Terror is a province with many caves. The birds and animals here are dangerous. The air here is filled with dangerous gases. The water is full of dead, floating dreams. The plants commonly found here are cactus and snakeroot. The most commonly found animal is the lizard which is also the Fear Monkey's best friend.

Anyone who stays in this land feels suffocated and contracts life-threatening diseases. People who lack resistance and willpower spend their entire lives in this land. This land is the root cause of stress in human lives.

Any human beings living here have a higher risk of obesity, heart problems, headaches, diabetes and anxiety.

Graves of past experiences are all over this land and prepared to haunt the Human Monkey if given the opportunity. The constantly moving spiders of worry are ready to take away the Human Monkey's peace of mind.

A person's deepest fears reside here in the Land of Terror.

The Human Monkey continued to walk in the lonely alleys and by-lanes of this land. At first, there was nothing but dark, black vacuum and the whispers of bats. He then observed a few skeletons that looked hauntingly familiar. But there was something peculiar about them: as soon as the Human Monkey moved towards them with a determined stride, they disappeared.

Fear disappears when we confront it and ask tough questions.

Even though all he could see around was darkness, the Human Monkey was determined and kept walking ahead.

Along the path, he saw shrivelled up, leafless trees and caves of all sizes.

The Human Monkey asked himself, 'Are you sure you want to go further?'

'Yes, one day or the other I will have to do this. Today is a good day as any,' said the voice inside.

There was an entire community of Fear Monkeys living in different caves. Some were in small caves and some in big ones! Small Fear Monkeys in small caves signify superficial fears that can be overcome easily, while giant Fear Monkeys in large caves are symbolic of deep-rooted and age-old fears.

A little ahead, the Human Monkey found a friend tied up to a big pillar right in the middle of the road. It was the Confidence Monkey. Alongside there were two other friends too who had been tied up—the Courage Monkey and the Confidence Monkey. The Human Monkey was puzzled. He had a lot of questions in his head and wanted to rescue all three of them. He tried talking to the Creative Monkey but couldn't get a word out. The Creative Monkey was afraid of guards coming and harming it.

It was night already and the Human Monkey knew that he did not have much time. Most Fear Monkeys sleep through the night but some of them prefer to work in the night. They are the ones giving us nightmares or popping up at that lonely hour just before it is time to wake up.

The Human Monkey then tried to speak to the Confidence Monkey.

When you are afraid, your confidence, creativity and courage get hijacked.

'Hey, please rescue me!' whispered the Confidence Monkey, looking around in fear.

'How did they get you?' asked the Human Monkey.

'I am not sure. There I was—a confident version of you—looking forward to the speech. Then suddenly, something crept up on me. It whispered into my ears the thought that there was a possibility that I could forget everything. That's all I remember before blacking out. When I woke up, I was here,' said the Confidence Monkey.

'You know something, I really miss you,' said the Human Monkey, sadly.

'I know that. It was me who helped you score great grades in Maths, it was me who helped you propose to Julia, and it was me who helped you excel in the sports camp during the last summer vacation. But after that, we met with an accident and since then, the Fear Monkeys kept shutting me up and now, they have kidnapped me,' said the emotional Confidence Monkey.

'Now I get it,' replied the Human Monkey. 'This is the reason I don't perform well any more. I hesitate to volunteer for anything, I stay away from taking initiative and I don't offer my opinion. I am also low all the time.'

'Yes, my brother!' said the Confidence Monkey, in a mournful tone, nodding furiously. Both the Courage Monkey and the Creativity Monkey were nodding too.

'So, how can I destroy the empire of the Fear Monkeys and take you all back with me right now? I want all of you back on my side. It was you, Creative Monkey, who helped me create an excellent design for last year's science project! It was you, Courage Monkey, who helped me raise my voice against injustice. Now, all of this is lost and I am left alone … sad and depressed!

'I want you all with me. I want to be happy! I want to be successful. I want to help people. I want to breathe freely. You guys wait here. I will immediately go and kill the Fear Monkeys once and for all.'

'No, no, you can't destroy them all at once. Even if you try, their master will come and hypnotise you. He has special powers and grows strong with every failure. But the reverse is also true.

'He is excellent at telling lies and trapping people. Close to 90 per cent of humans fall prey to Fear Monkeys. It is difficult to beat their arguments. They hypnotise people to give up on a lot of things. They influence us against investing, from going up on stage, against following our passions and from taking up any kind of risk.

'And if you disagree, they will show you the wall of misery. They will confuse you and prevent you from taking any step. And even if you do, they will be the poorly thought-through ones.'

'What's the wall of misery?' asked the Human Monkey out of curiosity.

'The Fear Monkeys used all those situations, where you were rejected, humiliated, ignored and when you failed, to build a wall, brick by brick. With every failure, this wall becomes bigger and stronger! All of us have it.'

'So, what's the way out? Can you tell me that?' the Human Monkey asked.

'No … I don't know the way out exactly. You can't destroy them immediately! You need to make a master plan to deal with them! The school library has a book called *The Lifeline* which holds the secret to dealing with the Fear Monkey. There are three families of Fear Monkeys. You will have to learn to deal with all three of them.'

## The Fear Monkey and his Families

The Human Monkey was taken aback when it heard that the Fear Monkey had three families. What could those three be, he wondered aloud. Pat came the reply from the Confidence Monkey.

The three families are:

1) The Insult-Proof Family
   They will make you avoid all the things that could hurt your ego.

2) The Dark Facts Family
   They will haunt you with past mistakes and future worries.

3) The Death-Proof Family
   These are good Fear Monkeys. The Human Monkey needs to use his judgement when dealing with them.

'Remember, not all of the Fear Monkeys are evil. Some are good for us too. We must learn to overpower only those monkeys who are not adding value to our life. I heard them say once that they are afraid of some 5-3-1 rule,' said the Confidence Monkey.

'What's this 5-3-1 rule?' asked the Human Monkey with curiosity.

'The 5-3-1 rule is a tool to destroy the Fear Monkey empire. I am not sure what it is. You have to find the book, understand it well and come up with a plan. I want to be with you always!' the Confidence Monkey replied.

The Human Monkey understood now that it was very important to recognise and accept the Fear Monkeys, and prepare a foolproof plan to deal with them.

The Human Monkey came back from the Land of Terror feeling quite excited about his decision to understand his own fears. He was now very certain that through a systematic process, he could gain control over the Fear Monkey. He also remembered the warning given by the Confidence Monkey—not to kill all the Fear Monkeys. Some of them are good for us, the Confidence Monkey had said. We only have to kill the unproductive ones.

The next day, the Human Monkey went to the library. He was a little worried about the availability of the book the Confidence Monkey had spoken about. Other students may have already had it issued, he thought and nervously asked the librarian for the book.

The librarian showed him where the book was located. As he made his way to the bookshelf, the Human Monkey was overcome by a feeling of curiosity. What was the 5-3-1 formula? Would it work?

Then he saw the book—*The Lifeline*.

Surprisingly, the book had not be issued in the last four years. If everyone has fears, then why aren't they trying to overcome them, he wondered.

The Human Monkey decided to pose this question to the Eagle of Wisdom at their next meeting. But for the moment, he was super-excited to read the book.

The Human Monkey learnt that originally, the Fear Monkey's job had been to protect us humans. This was when humans hadn't settled and had numerous threats to their lives. But the threats of modern day life are different. The Fear Monkey has started doing more harm than good in today's scenario by trying to protect us.

The three families of the Fear Monkey and the 5-3-1 rule were also mentioned in the book.

### The Insult-Proof Family

These monkeys will try to avoid all public embarrassment and are afraid of being judged. Furthermore, they are afraid of humiliation and rejection. They are constantly comparing you with others. They will want to keep you inside the caves forever so that nobody can ever make fun of you!

If you are very adamant about going and speaking to your latest crush, Anna, and if you think you should tell her that you like her, these monkeys will throw a googly in the form of destructive thoughts such as:

- You are overweight. Look at Anna! She is slim and tall.
- You look like a zombie, don't go!
- What if she slaps you right on your cheek!

Similarly, if you are part of a public gathering and want to speak up about something, these monkeys may start to say things like:

- It's not a good idea.
- People will laugh.
- What if you fumble?

This is perhaps the reason why public speaking is the #1 fear followed by death. The moment you decide to get up and speak in public, the Fear Monkey will start telling you all the possible things that could go wrong to protect from you from insult and humiliation.

Three out of four people suffer from speech anxiety. This monkey is successful in paralysing performance, which is accompanied by an immediate variety of physical and emotional symptoms. These symptoms interfere in the person's ability to successfully give a speech or make a presentation. They include anxiety, worry, nervousness, trembling, sweating, dizziness and so on.

These are the monkeys which prevent you from going up in public. They attempt to avoid a public appearance at any cost.

If you have any of the fears mentioned below, then you are probably a victim of the Insult-Proof family of monkeys:

- Fear of expressing your point of view
- Fear of questioning
- Fear of speaking in mass gatherings
- Fear of asking about your rights

The Insult-Proof family will never let you speak. To express opinions, you need to be free, and your mental space has to be utilised for preparing not for panicking.

## How to deal with the Insult-Proof Family?

(Note: Don't fight with them! Fighting with them will multiply their strength! Yes, they do reproduce fast!)

There are five rules for dealing with these monkeys. The final and most important one will help you reach the Purple Island.

## Rule 1: Offer cherries to these monkeys

Let us suppose that you are walking upstairs. You don't know yet but there is a lizard on the twelfth step which you will notice only when you reach the eighth step.

Now, after spotting the thick, fat, brown, spotted hazel-eyed lizard, within a tenth of a second, the lizard's image is transferred from the retina to the brain. And, it takes you another tenth of a second to realise that it may spit poison at you. Another tenth of a second to realise that since you have to go upstairs for a scheduled meeting, you can't create a scene.

And if you have a phobia of lizards, this is a really tough situation. But, suddenly, you get a call from a friend saying that a common friend has broken up with her boyfriend of nine years. Even as you are processing this, you get a message from another person indicating that you are required at the meeting upstairs quickly. You then calmly and quickly walk up those stairs, past the lizard, without batting an eyelid!

Now what happened here?

1. The call from your friend diverted your attention.
2. Due to the change in focus, your body stopped releasing the stress hormone.
3. You were quite shocked to hear of your friend's break-up. Technically, you were distracted, and that made you walk up those stairs without worrying too much about the lizard.

This is what I mean by giving cherries to the monkeys. The Fear Monkey will keep eating those cherries and you can go about your work. There is nothing better than keeping the anxious monkey distracted.

Distraction methods:

1. Anxious? Distract yourself with a game.
2. Afraid? Give yourself a surprise.
3. Surprise is food for all the monkeys. While they are playing with it, the Human Monkey can quickly finish work.

So, when I say feed the monkeys with cherries, I actually mean, surprise them!

**Rule 2: Let me see what happens next**

Accept the fears. Don't argue.

By arguing, you may actually be helping the reason that the Fear Monkey is proposing to become stronger. He will show you the Wall of Misery that will demonstrate the umpteen number of times that things did not work out for you.

Instead, motivate yourself by saying that you are ready for a new challenge. Just try to let go and get excited about what's in store next. 'Let's see what happens next,' is a good mantra to live by.

**Rule 3: The 'I am not alone' mantra**

*I have a superpower. I am not alone.*

So the next time you are afraid of walking alone on the path of uncertainty, wary of taking that tough decision or just working yourself up about giving a big public talk, taking that business risk or speaking out to your loved ones about a sensitive issue, just remind yourself, 'I am not alone.' You can pray and recall the God you worship.

Prayers have an important significance in life.

I am not alone!
I am not alone!
I am not alone!

Try it for the first three times and you will find that the Fear Monkey is already becoming weaker.

Attempt number 1: You will be very, very afraid!
Attempt number 2: You will be very afraid.
Attempt number 3: You will be slightly afraid.
Attempt number 4: The Fear Monkey starts to become weaker and weaker.

**Point to Note:** You only have to show willpower for the first two to three times. Any task is frightening at the start. Later, it becomes easy.

**Rule 4: Set a timer**

The next time the Fear Monkey comes and hampers your attempt, stop and set a timer!

**Fear Monkey:** Oh, don't speak in between! They are really big shots. They will never consider your idea.

Start your mental timer—tick, tick ...

**Human Monkey:** Okay, what else?

**Fear Monkey:** He is the president of the company. Your idea of improving sales is stupid and it will take you nowhere. They will laugh at you ... probably humiliate you in front of these VIPs.

**Human Monkey:** Okay, you have been speaking for the last fifteen seconds ... what else do you want to say? Speak up, I am giving you time.

**Fear Monkey:** Speaking about this idea can turn into your worst nightmare ... they might just throw you out of the company! You will lose your job.

**Human Monkey:** Ask him, 'How will I lose my job by speaking about this idea?'
**Fear Monkey:** Umm ... I don't know!

Then the Fear Monkey stops nagging you.

Just accept whatever it is saying and go and do what you feel is right. Setting a timer and accepting whatever the Fear Monkey is saying for a brief interval is a good idea. Let him speak but don't agree with what he has to say. There is always a difference between accepting and agreeing.

Believe that you are not alone and just do it!

Yes, just do it and finish it.

You will feel a lot better.

And act fast.

The Fear Monkey is afraid of quick actions. He can't think that fast.

**Rule 5: The Purple Island.**
This place has the power to instantly nullify all the Fear Monkeys. We will learn all about this island a little later.

## The Dark Fact Family

The Dark Fact Monkeys will remind you about all the past experiences where you failed and thus prevent you from taking a step ahead. Your past failures are the dark facts that they cling to.

Did you go through a failure in the past that haunts you even today and affects your ability to make a decision? If yes, you are a victim of the Dark Fact family of monkeys.

There are three rules for dealing with these monkeys.

**Rule 1: Throw some oxygen bars at them**

The minute you see that your Fear Monkey is growing stronger and beginning to give you panic attacks, resort to using oxygen bars. They will help the Human Monkey take control.

But what are they? Oxygen bars are nothing but deep breaths. And there are many different techniques of taking deep breaths, all of which are equally powerful.

You can start with simple Anulom-Vilom pranayama, Bhramari or something even simpler. You could keep it uncomplicated and go for the good, old-fashioned deep breath, too!

How many oxygen bars? It depends on the dominance of the Fear Monkey at that point of time. If it is hyperactive you may need to take around ten or more oxygen bars at frequent intervals.

These deep breaths release good chemicals called endorphins and soon, the Fear Monkey becomes inactive!

On the contrary when you are stressed, cortisol, the stress hormone is released which is responsible for fear and anxiety.

**Rule 2: Light the Candle of Hope**

Certain negative experiences from the past can have a powerful impact on a person. In such a situation, logical reasoning may not be very helpful. During these times, use the power of hope.

Imagine that you are holding a candle and it is taking you towards light. That candle is helping you find the right path.

Hope has cured many diseases, resolved many difficult situations and won many arguments. A person with hope can go a long way.

**Rule 3: Take him for a walk.**

Ask the Dark Fact Monkey questions. Speak to him gently. Try to resolve the matter in your own head.

Recall the past incident and try to understand why it still haunts you. Is it really that scary? Or have you just created a mountain out of a molehill?

## The Death-Proof Family

This family of monkeys is the onc that tells you to be afraid of all kinds of heights, water, speed, fire, health hazards and so on.

To deal with these monkeys, you will need to use the Key of Judgement i.e. your own judgement.

For instance, when a person is afraid of elevators or flying, it's actually the Fear Monkey that is afraid of accidents. But is there really something to be afraid of? This is what the person has to decide, based on the facts in front of him.

Similarly, if you are afraid of going for a swim in a lake which might land you in trouble, then it's a good fear.

So, it's all about thinking and using your right judgement when dealing with this fear.

And this, my friends, is the 5-3-1 rule.

| *Insult Proof Family* | *Dark Fact Family* | *Death Proof Family* |
|---|---|---|
| Give them cherries | | |
| Let me see what happens next! | Throw some oxygen bars | |
| I am not alone! | Light the Candle of Hope | Use judgement |
| Set a timer | Take him for a walk | |
| Wait for Purple Island! | | |

These are the key solutions. But the ultimate solution lies in the Purple Island.

**Points to remember:**

1. Fear is good and bad. Our mind secretes fear hormones to protect us from danger. That's fine, because it wants to keep us alive.
2. But constant, pointless fear is deadly to have.
3. When in fear, divert your mind. Don't give your mind space to think about the fear. Keep yourself busy.
4. When afraid, start breathing deeply!
5. Always carry a candle of hope! When in doubt just believe that everything will be fine!
6. Take deliberate action the first three times, the fourth time you will see it pay off.

# The Drunk Monkey ... The Monkey That Changes Colours!

The P-Monkey places huge obstacles in your path. The Fear Monkey damages your soul by restricting your choices and risk-taking ability. The wild Drunk Monkey damages your relationships and ruins the quality of your life.

The Drunk Monkey is different. This monkey can change his form in a fraction of second. The most important thing to understand about this monkey is that he is very difficult to find. Sometimes, he is to be found in the cleanest of places and at other times, he hangs around in messy locations. Sometimes, he can be seen with people engaging in spiritual discussions and at others he might be found talking ill about a work colleague. He is happy and grateful at times and cranky and complaining at others. The Drunk Monkey is capable of confusing you completely or making you think clearly. You may appear to be a wonderful human being on some days and an annoying beast on others depending on the Drunk Monkey's mood.

This monkey is a great believer in tit for tat. Let's understand it through a situation. Your roommate has had a bad day and is therefore not in a talkative mood. The Drunk

Monkey will tell you to show your roommate the same kind of behaviour on subsequent days. If your roommate behaved arrogantly, you respond with arrogance. If they acted selfishly, you will also demonstrate selfishness.

### How to Identify the Drunk Monkey

Have you ever been in a situation where you reacted to something or someone and then regretted it? Have you said yes to a deal because you got excited at that moment and later thought it was a poor decision? Have you abused someone and later wondered whether the situation that prompted it was actually your fault and not the other person's? Have you displayed a lot of attitude in a relationship, although your intention was to respond to these situations in a healthy or mature way?

Controlling oneself in a situation is not something everyone can manage. Often, instead of responding, we react. And react badly! Not only does it exhaust and irritate us but also the people around us. There are several situations where we do things at the spur of the moment and regret every second of it later.

It is pretty similar to a drunk person acting up under the influence of alcohol and then wondering the next day why he did what he did.

Some more examples:

1. Your intention is to save money. But in the heat of the moment you blow it all away in buying a dress that you hardly wear now!

2. You had every intention of seriously listening to your brother talk about his business idea. But something took over and you reacted funnily making your brother think that you were rude and selfish.
3. Your in-laws think you are difficult because of your quick temper! You are unable to control even it though you want to.
4. There are days when you clean up your entire room and resolve to keep it that way going forward. Then you receive a call that puts you in a negative mood and your resolution crashes!
5. Last night you over-committed your contribution for a party, and now you are wondering why you did that.

Thank the Drunk Monkey for all these situations. It is the driver of human emotions and loves to take the lead. Our first reactions are usually the Drunk Monkey's responses.

A human being displays a variety of contrasting emotions: happy-sad, grateful-complaining, caring-jealous, secure-insecure, love-hate and so on. Emotions are natural and spontaneous. It is normal for human beings to experience contrasting emotions through the day.

But what many of us lack is the control over these emotions. We feel that they just happen. That's the Drunk Monkey at work—your emotions just 'happening'. High performers, on the other hand, know exactly how to deal with this monkey.

In my last book, *Think and Win like Dhoni*, the crux was how M.S. Dhoni keeps calm, handles pressure and acts against his wild monkeys to allow his best judgement behaviour to prevail.

Dealing with this monkey can take us ahead in life. The Eagle of Wisdom says, if this monkey becomes your friend, the world is yours!

You will be the master of your own emotions and know how to drive the mind to perform optimally when required!

You will know when to increase your speed, when to slow down and relax, when to stay calm and when to react. But more importantly, you will not just 'know' but also be able to 'apply' this knowledge.

People talk of 'knowing' what is good for them, but not being able to actually act upon it. The simple solution to that is being able to control your Drunk Monkey!

How? Read on.

Let's do a small check! Analyse the week that went by and figure out all the possible emotions you felt during the course of the week.

1. You might have been very happy when your boss praised you, or vice-versa.
2. You might have felt grateful about having a loving family. Maybe you had a difference of opinion with your family and you complained that they didn't understand you.
3. Did you feel superior about your work and position? Or did you feel inferior when you saw someone in a better position than you?
4. Did you feel excited and joyful about something good that happened or were you cranky about the rain and traffic jam?

As stated previously, we feel a variety of emotions throughout the day. Some emotions are good and keep us healthy while some are dangerous because they are a cause of misery.

Let's discuss some good emotions. They are the ones that make you smile, sing, love, laugh and dance! I am sure you must have experienced happiness on seeing a cute baby and felt overjoyed on hearing news of your promotion. You were probably passionate about marrying the person you love, grateful for the family you have and so on.

We also experience anger on seeing a person ill-treated, frustration when things don't go our way and many other such emotions.

All these and more are the shades of the Drunk Monkey.

But why are we calling the monkey 'drunk'? Because these monkeys are subconscious observers. The Drunk Monkey concocts a cocktail of the behaviour and attitudes it observes and they determine its mood at the moment.

## The Many Shades of the Drunk Monkey

The Drunk Monkey can be broadly classified into two: the Green Drunk Monkey and the Red Drunk Monkey. While they are twins, they are complete opposites.

The Green Drunk Monkey is subtle, soft and joyful. The Red Drunk Monkey is responsible for anger, ego, jealousy, hatred and all the negative emotions we experience.

We must try and be in the company of the Green Monkey as far as possible. It will help us feel good, understand people better and improve the quality of life in general. Here's how the Green Monkey makes you feel:

1. **Miss Grateful:** She reminds you to be thankful for who you are and all that you have. How blessed you are to read this book with two eyes. How fortunate you are to get food every single day. How privileged you are to be alive. To feel grateful is to feel whole and to possess the ability to attract whatever you love.

But, it is incredibly difficult to feel grateful always. Wild monkeys forever attack you when you are in this blissful state. Fighting these monkeys off is quite a task.

But how do you prevent the monkeys from showing up? Wait … for THE PURPLE ISLAND!

2. **Mr Secure:** It provides the Human Monkey a sense of assurance on being free from danger—whether emotional or physical. Without it, the Human Monkey feels insecure.
3. **Miss Hopeful:** Hope is what lends substance to our existence. It offers us reasons to live, work and dream. Often people lose hope and give up on life. But it is important to know that with self-affirmation and self-belief, hope can always come back.
4. **Mr Passionate:** Passion is the adrenaline coursing through your veins giving you the energy to outperform competition. Passion is a necessary ingredient for achieving greatness.

5. **Miss Charming:** Creativity, charm and being vibrant are essential to lead an interesting life. Dullness has no place in Miss Charming's domain.

Let's understand the Red Monkey better.

The Red Monkey doesn't just represent anger. This monkey also makes the person egoistic, hateful, complaining, irritating and much more. Have you seen these kind of people? Yes, their Red Monkey dominates them completely. Let's see how dangerous this monkey is!

1. **Mr Sad:** Sadness is the primary reason for the birth of other negative monkeys. It must be kept away at all costs. Sadness is too high a price to pay for anything in life.
2. **Miss Ego:** This monkey wants to be in control all the time. This monkey likes nothing better than being right all the time. She aspires to outperform anyone who comes in her path and is responsible for destroying relationships.

3. **Mr Hate:** Hate gets activated when the ego becomes insecure. Hate destroys everything in its path and is the cause of damaging human behaviour.
4. **Mr Judgement:** Passing judgement on others is routine for this monkey. Consider these statements:
   'She is too skinny!'
   'Celebrities must be very arrogant!'
   'News channels are forever showing paid news.'
   In the fight happening at the neighbours', the mother-in-law is right.
   'Why is she wearing a blazer? Can't she dress properly?'

These are some instances of unwarranted judgement that he keeps passing. It occupies a lot of mental space and prevents us from doing any actual work. Criticism is a close cousin of this monkey.

5. **Miss Comparison:** Comparisons with others is this monkey's favourite pastime. You will find her frivolous in disposition and usually a scatterbrain. She is outwardly bubbly and very insecure within. With comparison comes misery closely followed by complaints. The Complaint Monkey is Miss Comparison's constant companion.
6. **Mr Revenge:** Plotting revenge on those who have supposedly 'humiliated' you is this monkey's hobby. Rather than focusing on the present, the Revenge Monkey will keep reminding you of the past and cook up plots to right wrongs.

The Green Monkey helps you see clearly, plan wisely and supports you in healthy decision making. The Red Monkey completely blurs your vision, clutters your plans and provokes you to make poor decisions. Clearly, a green signal from the Green Monkey and a red signal from the Red Monkey will result in very different behaviour.

Let's look at scenarios to understand the difference in behaviour when the Green Monkey is dominant as opposed to the Red Monkey and vice versa.

### Scenario I

Your mother says, 'It's not safe to stay out late. Please be back in time.'

The Green Monkey's reaction is likely to be, 'Okay, she said that because she cares about me. I must understand her intentions.'

The security aspect is activated (Mr Secure).

The Red Monkey's reaction is likely to be very different. He is likely to say, 'Why is this woman interfering. I can take care of myself! I am an independent woman.'

The ego aspect is activated (Miss Ego).

### Scenario II

Your friend wants to borrow a dress for a party.

She says, 'Hey, I really liked your pink choker dress. Can I borrow it for a party?'

If you are in a good mood and the Green Monkey is active, the response is likely to be, 'Yes, of course, you can take it. How can I forget how much you cared for me when I was sick!'

The grateful part of the personality is activated.

The Red Monkey is likely to make us react differently. It will probably worry about your friend getting all the attention and prompt you to refuse.

### Scenario III

Your boyfriend and you decide to meet for coffee. He is late because of a traffic jam. The Green Monkey would take it in his stride and do something else till he arrives. But the Red Monkey is likely to get harried and plot revenge, or make a mental note to be late the next time 'to teach him a lesson'.

Here are a few ways in which you can handle the Red Monkey.

1. Whenever you find that anger, hate or for that matter any negative emotion is overpowering you, try and first observe it from a safe distance. Let your Human Monkey analyse all the signals that have triggered off these emotions. A person should be able to determine what makes him angry, hateful, egoistic and so on. If anger is what you feel, ask yourself, how long do you

generally stay angry? Ten minutes? Forty minutes? Two hours? Two days? List down the things that make you angry.

1. ________________________________
2. ________________________________
3. ________________________________

Similarly you can write down your list for other 'red' emotions too!

Identify the emotion and figure out how to deal with it.

2. As mentioned in the chapter on the Fear Monkey, feeding cherries may be a good way to distract the Drunk Monkeys too. Divert their attention to something that is surprising or consumes more attention.
3. Avoid the company of people who have a tendency to speak negatively or those who make you feel miserable. Hang out with people who have a fresh and optimistic way of looking at life. Be in the company of those who value you, will enrich your experience and offer you strength and confidence. This will make the Green Monkey show up more often.
4. Relax and learn to let go. Things like traffic jams, power cuts, internet troubles so on are beyond our control. There are times when have to stop taking life so seriously, accept things as they are and let go. Sometimes you have tell yourself that things are okay and it's just a phase!

**Points to remember:**

1. Drunk Monkeys are the various human emotions.
2. If we are happy, positive emotions and actions follow, but the reverse is also true.
3. On a bad day or during a bad phase, your reactions seem to change. This is when we can try specific ways to deal with them.
4. They can be eradicated but you have to be very consistent in your approach!

# When the Monkeys Attack Together

To deal with one monkey attacking you is relatively easy. But, what do you do when they attack in a troop? And that's often how it is in day-to-day life. The strength of the tribe grows manifold with the monkeys feeding off each other, rendering you powerless.

Let's consider a scenario.

### Scenario I

It's the beginning of the month. Your salary has just been credited and you are out window-shopping. At least, that's what you tell yourself. Your Human Monkey reminds you at the beginning of your shopping expedition, 'You will not shop. You will save money this month and in the months to come, to buy your dream car.'

As you walk around the mall, confident in your resolve, you spot something in a shop window—that magical dress that you must have! You walk up to it. Only looking, you tell yourself. The Human Monkey senses that things aren't looking good and it reminds you again, 'You have enough clothes for the moment. Save money! Remember! Save!'

You look at the price. It's steep and will result in a big hole in your savings plan. It's definitely not for you. You are about to walk away when a thought occurs, 'Maybe, I could try it on and click a selfie. No harm in that!'

You step into the store and pick up the dress from its rack. The Human Monkey raises his voice, 'This is what you do all the time. Do you know how much you have to work to earn what you do?'

Then, the P-Monkey steps in, 'You have a great deal of work waiting for you back at home. Enjoy your leisure. A selfie. Maybe two. That's it! You have plenty of time tomorrow to work. Today, enjoy your break.'

Now it's the Drunk Monkey's turn to contribute to the discussion. 'It's been a long day. You are entitled to some stress relief. Go ahead. Wear that dress. Click that selfie. Enjoy this moment.'

It's almost as if the Drunk Monkey and the P-Monkey are talking to each other. The Human Monkey is attempting to get things back on track, but failing.

**P-Monkey:** 'I am just trying the dress on!'
**Human Monkey:** 'Why? We have a lot of work at home!'
**P-Monkey:** 'Wow, it looks very good! This is awesome. You could wear it to your next conference. You will look amazing!'

The Human Monkey is frustrated!

The Drunk Monkey is observing all of this and waiting for the right time to make his move.

**Drunk Monkey:** 'Life is short. You should enjoy every moment and what will you do with all these savings if you don't know how to enjoy today. Buy this dress. Look, there's a discount on it too.'

**P-Monkey:** Yes. Do it. Buy this dress and enjoy the evening. Tomorrow, you have to get back to work. Not today. Tomorrow!

What happens next is anyone's guess. You buy the dress, the Human Monkey is silenced and the savings plan is pushed for 'later'.

### A Few More Scenarios

1. 'I won't write a new book because I am afraid it will fail.'

At first sight, it appears that this is clearly the Fear Monkey attacking you. Pause and think again. It is also the P-Monkey who simply doesn't want to work. The duo, a deadly combination, are working together to come up with excuses on why you shouldn't work.

2. 'My cousin humiliated me the last time we met. Not this time! I will teach him a lesson!'

This isn't an uncommon scenario. Somebody tried to put you down. You are upset and want to settle scores. Both the Ego Monkey and the Revenge Monkey are set to work together to blind Human Monkey's vision.

Pause. Recognise that it is your Drunk Monkey that's acting up. First, try and understand why the person behaved the way they did. Perhaps their Drunk Monkey was acting up?

Secondly, ask if it really was humiliation? Maybe he meant something else and you misunderstood. But your Ego Monkey and Revenge Monkey are making you think otherwise and gunning for retribution.

Finally, analyse your response to all these questions and evaluate your Drunk Monkey. Make a conscious decision.

**How do you deal with a combined monkey attack?**

1. Observe: Firstly, understand and label the monkeys. Write down your current challenges and try to figure out which monkeys are responsible.
2. Once you know what monkeys are at work, decide which one you want to tackle first. We have discussed strategies like feeding cherries, lighting up the Candle of Hope, taking the monkey for a walk and so on. Choose the option that seems best suited.
3. Even if you are dealing with one monkey at a time, make sure to handle all of them. Don't take care of just one monkey and ignore the rest. To ignore one of them is to leave the door half-open for the monkeys to get together and stage another attack.

But there is one place where these monkeys cannot attack you, where you can live without fear of being overpowered by them. The Purple Island. Now before the P-Monkey tells you to put down this boring book and look for something else more exciting, let us go to the Purple Island. Let's experience this ultimate space.

# The Purple Island

You have problems in life?

You have this one particular problem which has occupied your mental space. It has taken away your liveliness and what not!

Before you think more about it, hang on!

Just close your eyes and use your biggest weapon!

Biggest Weapon?

Yes! Many don't realise it! And I don't know if you have realised it yet!

Alright, let's do it together. If you are reading this, just keep everything aside and take a long and deep breath. Breathe in till the oxygen goes down to your abdomen, filling in all the space. And then breathe out slowly till you feel completely empty. Imagine yourself feeling empty. That's important!

Close your eyes and allow yourself three such long breaths.

Now did you feel the cold whirlpool of energy? A soothing balm of serenity? A calming nothingness that settles you from within?

That's the Purple Island for you!

The Purple Island is the 'present land which should be the home of Human Monkey'.

Take a moment and just think about it! Create your own purple island. The only catch here is that it should look purple!

This is where Human Monkey should stay. But with day-to-day challenges, the Human Monkey is forced to stay with the Fear Monkey, the Ego Monkey, the Sad Monkey and others. Everyday, we are so exhausted with day-to-day things that we hardly notice the many miracles that are happening around us.

The Purple Island is a zone where magic does happen. But are you trained enough to see the magic? That's the big question.

### What this Island can do for you

Here, on this island, a person's focus multiplies, worries divide, the past gets subtracted and stillness and calm are continuously added. People become creative and new ideas and solutions are constantly pouring out. And why the purple colour? You will know that soon!

On this island, all the good monkeys become active and the wild monkeys lose their power, or fall in line with your dream. Yes, they use their power to fuel your dream. For example, a Fear Monkey is bad when he is not letting you perform, but he is good when he keeps you away from danger.

On the Purple Island, the Fear Monkey will be active only to avoid danger. The Procrastinator Monkey will procrastinate only on the things which are unimportant. The Drunk Monkey will work for you. There will be moments of anger, but only for constructive reasons. There will be confusion, but only for you to make better choices.

Here on this island, champions are made! Warriors are born! This island can turn the unfortunate to fortunate, the sick to healthy and the clueless into a wise one. It is because the purple sand here doesn't allow wild monkeys to swing and somersault, but makes them stay focused and co-operate.

People here love to wake up with that bright smile of ease, and be aware that they have twenty-four hours added in their account to live fully and cultivate the gems of passion and hard work. The people here truly listen to all kind of sounds because they are attentive as the wild monkeys don't dance. They can recognise the sound of a chirping bird, the sound of a baby's laughter, the sound of waves, the sound of trees… Here, everyone understands that the true gift of life is this moment, and everything else is an assumption based on experience.

### How can you spend maximum time on Purple Island?

As the Human Monkey walked around the Purple Island, he took in its many sights—its pristine air scented with mogra flowers, the soothing breeze, bright sunlight and most of all, its many purple lotuses.

The island was full of purple lotuses of compassion, purple birds of positivity, the purple air of stillness and in fact, the purple cold breeze which is as powerful as the sword!

Even as he was mulling over this, for the first time he paid attention to the little purple birds which he sees everyday but never paid attention to!

He saw purple lilies dancing in the breeze. This moment filled him with pure love and he experienced a stillness. He experienced his own presence at this moment. His attention went to each cell of his body and he saw life! Miss Gratitude came in from somewhere and sat on his shoulder. He never understood what happened.

Whenever he breathed in the purple breeze, he felt as though every cell had washed itself and rejuvenated itself with pure stillness. He realised that whatever had happened in the past had happened just to bring him to this moment. He was happy with the past now and had made peace with it.

He understood the depth of his dream and sensed the power of his vision. He felt light as a feather and as powerful as a sword. He came into contact with a new, fresh perspective of life.

The Human Monkey then spotted an old resident. He appeared to be a happy soul with bright fierce eyes, a sharp pointed nose and a radiant pink face. The persona of this man was extremely powerful and strong.

He thought to himself, 'Though he is old, he looks fresh.'

This was the first person he saw on the Purple Island.

Intrigued, the Human Monkey asked him the question he had been dying to ask, 'Hi Sir, I am new to this land. How can I spend my maximum time on this land?'

The senior resident replied, 'Oh, I am so glad that you want to live here. Atleast you found this place, otherwise today's generation is very far from this place. They are almost unaware that it exists and I doubt they will ever discover this land. They will always keep running behind material wealth and fall short because with just material wealth it is impossible to obtain true success. This is the only reason why human beings have started falling ill and getting hideous diseases early in life inspite of advanced medical science and technology. Now that you are here, I will tell you the ways to do well in your personal and professional life.'

### Rules to Stay on at the Purple Island!

1. Steal the remote control.

   The Human Monkey didn't understand what this meant at first. The senior resident then asked him to make a list of people on whom his happiness depended.

   Let's write the names of people on whom our happiness depends!

   1. ______________________
   2. ______________________
   3. ______________________
   4 ______________________

All these people have the secret remote to control you. Take that remote back. Once you snatch the remote back, you will have full control and now you can activate the monkey you want.

Once you are in control, it's all up to you. If you feel you are getting complacent, you could activate the good Fear Monkey. He will make you come on track. If you feel your Ego Monkey is taking control, you could activate feeling grateful. You could always keep Confidence Monkey with you and keep your passion fires burning.

2. Wear a 'Thank you' and 'Sorry' label.
   The senior resident said, 'I saw many people in my lifetime for whom their pride and ego were the biggest things. They keep feeding the Ego Monkey by taking credit all the time, by putting others down and by not being open to listening. This leads to poor relationships, which is a permanent invitation to sadness.

'Thank you' and 'Sorry' are two words which will keep your Ego Monkey in control. And trust me, when it is controlled, half the problems are solved!

To stay on this island you should be humble enough to accept your mistakes. To stay on this island you should be grateful enough to digest criticism. Good and bad are just labels. Without these two labels, your Ego Monkey will remain active and once it is active, your exit from the Purple island is guaranteed. Once a person start being humble and grateful, the Ego Monkey will stop growing. He will not get his food and eventually he will shrink because of starving.'

3. Expect less and execute more.
   The senior citizen also added, 'You have to focus more on work and expect less from results. Here Fear Monkey will fool you. You have to beware of him. If you keep thinking and worry about the results ... you won't get there! A lot of your time will just go into analysis which will lead to stress. You will feel like you worked enough when you hardly worked! You need to execute more and it automatically takes up

your chances to qualify for better results. Most people keep getting stressed about the future and then they are again thrown out of Purple Island.'

Listening to all this, the Human Monkey started believing in the process rather than overstressing about the results. He wanted to make himself more capable and a doer than just a wishful thinker!

4. Use the monkey-numbering meditation technique. Now this meditation technique is also called as 'thought numbering meditation' as each monkey comes up with a thought. When you label and count them, you can actually separate your thoughts and choose the best one for you!

   Meditation releases the feel-good hormone called serotonin and oxytocin which are responsible for lifting the mood. It will help all the good monkeys to take control. Oxytocin is a love and caring hormone and will make you empathetic.

Stress, on the other hand, leads to the monkeys dancing and this dance lead to the release of cortisol, a stress hormone. When you meditate periodically, good hormones are released and it is a sure way to continue staying on the Purple Island. Even if Wild Monkeys try to pull you out, you will have the power to kill them.

If you are new to meditation, start with short durations. But make sure you are consistent with it. Don't let the P-Monkey interfere and distract you.

5. Pretend you are wearing an invisible Purple Crown. Look around and try to spot the colour purple. Let the purple colour be a gentle reminder for you to be in the Purple Island. Try and feel that there is purple energy on your head asking you to be cool, relaxed and effective. This is your Purple Crown.

Start reminding yourself about the Purple Crown every day. Once you subsequently make it a habit, you will be more effective in your work. It's not the crown which is changing you. It's the attitude that it engenders in you.

# A Few Months Later

The Human Monkey got back his remote from all the people on whom his happiness depended. He started being happy most of the time. He began to notice a great amount of creativity in his work. He always kept an eye out for the invisible Purple Crown. He did not dwell much upon others' opinions, though he did listen to everything carefully without judgment. He planned his work and gave his 100 per cent without worrying about the results.

He got up every morning and finished his daily morning rituals. He breathes the purple breeze regularly. He participated in all sorts of activities and finished every assignment on time. Life was smooth.

The Human Monkey also discovered that with every wild monkey he dropped, a new world opened up.

One fine day, he came across his old friend, the Eagle.

'What are you doing here?' asked the Human Monkey.

'I live here,' replied the Eagle.

'What? You live here?' The Human Monkey was surprised.

'All animals stay here. It's humans who find it difficult to stay here. Maybe because they don't follow the rules.'

The Eagle further added, 'Let me tell you, the Purple Island is not a physical land. It is the moment you are in right now! In fact, it's a land on which your existence depends! If the land slides, your physical existence ends! Think about it! This Island can give you everything, but only if you value it and only if you manage to stay on it. Apart from this Island every other place is full of trouble. Try living in the Ego Monkey's house or for that matter in the house of Revenge, Fear or Anger and you will suffer!'

The Eagle continued, 'The present island is the most beautiful. It's the actual Heaven! In fact, Hell and Heaven are what you create! Hell is when you are overpowered by wild monkeys and start to complain, start being ungrateful and start to crib. Heaven is when you control your monkeys, learn to be at peace inspite of tough situations'

The Eagle let his message sink in before speaking further. 'Why the name Purple Island? The purple colour is a signal to live in the present moment. It is purple because it brings balance of blue and red. The purple colour is obtained by mixing the blue and red colours. Red brings intensity and energy to the colour and blue brings stability and relaxation. Together they become purple which is a perfect balance of these two.'

The Human Monkey then asked, 'But if the Purple Island is the very place, the very moment that I live in, then why don't I live in it every day?'

The Eagle of Wisdom smiled. 'Because your Wild Monkeys also have a life! They also want to live! And they don't want to die like that!'

The Human Monkey then asked, 'But what if the Wild Monkeys haunt me again and take me to their land? I am not sure how long I will stay here?'

'Then again come back to the Purple Island!! Keep your Confidence Monkey on one shoulder and Miss Grateful on other. They will help you control your wild monkey. You can also use a variety of techniques. Use the Candle of Hope when you are afraid, shut the Drunk Monkey up when it attacks, use the reverse engineering technique when the P-Monkey is on the prowl and so on. You know all of them. *The fact that you realised that they are monkeys and not you means half the battle is won.*'

'Eagle, a last question please?' requested the Human Monkey.

'What about that message which I saw often, but couldn't decode what it meant? I feel something for a moment whenever I see this message and then that feeling vanishes!'

(The jumbled message 'nay ady acn eb het alts yad!' which was mentioned at the beginning of the book on Page 10.)

In a flash, the Eagle rearranged the jumbled English letters and read, '*Any day can be the last day!*'

The Human Monkey smiled. He had understood what he had to do.

He was ready to face the world.

His new life began.

## Points to Remember

1. 'Any day can be the last day!' Don't forget that fact.
2. The present moment will automatically push the wild monkeys aside.
3. Only your confidence and gratefulness will be with you in the present.
4. Whenever you feel, you are surrounded by the monkeys the first thing is to come into the present moment. It has all the solutions. *Try!*

# A Personal Note

How are you doing?

I hope you have recognised your inner monkeys and begun controlling the wild ones.

A suggestion: for one week just attempt to recognise the presence of the wild monkeys. Once you are able to recognise them, you are a step ahead and they will automatically start to lose their power. From there on, move one step at a time to work towards controlling them.

Life is beautiful and it is up to us to choose to see it. Let that choice stay with us and not with our unwanted emotions.

I have made a list of a few thought branches that these monkeys keep swinging to and fro from all day. They will help you understand which monkey is attacking you and how you can respond to them.

Please write to me with your experiences with these monkeys over email: meet.sfurtisahare@gmail.com

Or find me on Instagram at 'sfurtisahare'.

**A Few Daily Situations**

1. Neha decides to start work on her assignments before the deadline. While using the washroom, she checks her face. A voice pops up, 'My double chin is quite visible. How did I become so fat? I look miserable. Also, I am not that tall and I have pimples on my face too.'

   Neha … WAITTTTT! You are complaining.

   **Solution:** Bring Miss Grateful into the picture and think of the things you have. You have a fully functional heart, liver, kidneys and other body parts. Be grateful for them. Don't take them for granted.

2. While preparing for your presentation, you suddenly start to think about what could go wrong when you are making the presentation. These thoughts haunt you:

   'What if they ask me this question?'

   'What if the slides don't change when I want them to?'

   Wait … wait. Your Fear Monkey is trying to dominate you.

   **Solution:** Make yourself strong. Bring in the Confidence Monkey and recall your last big win. Take a deep breath and use the mantra, 'Let me see what happens next!'

3. Anna bagged a business deal. In that moment of victory, her thoughts start with 'Wow, I am so happy.

Finally, my hardwork has paid off!' and then move to, 'Now I will show him how good I am. Last year he had said I was useless. Let me show this idiot!'

Wait ... wait, that's not you. It's your Revenge Monkey showing up.

**Solution:** Remind yourself that the Revenge Monkey is just trying to misguide your focus. You may not realise it now but it will impact you in the long run. Forget the past, focus on the present and learn to be more empathetic.

4. You are trying to call someone dear to you. The phone's busy. You start to wonder, 'Whom is he speaking to? What if he is seeing someone else? Is he cheating on me?' Your thoughts then move to, 'Let me teach him a lesson. I will make him realise, how it feels when the phone is on wait for half-an-hour.'

   Wait ... wait ... Your Revenge Monkey and Fear Monkey are attacking together.

   **Solution:** It is quite natural to feel trapped when two monkeys attack you simultaneously.

   In this case, first kill the Fear Monkey using the Candle of Hope. The Candle of Hope will bring back your trust and help you believe that everything is and will be alright.

5. Your boss says, 'You are not prepared for this position now. You probably need to wait for six more months.'

   Your thoughts go, 'How dare she! Me? Unprepared? Who is she? She doesn't know me. I have always been a topper. I have been a gold medallist at my university.'

Wait ... wait ... Your Ego Monkey is showing up.

**Solution:** Knowing that the Ego Monkey is likely to crop up in this situation and ruin everything, try and find a solution before that can happen. A massive ego is a big roadblock in enjoying the small things that life has to offer.

Let us look at a few more scenarios and possible solutions that you could use to tame the monkey of the moment!

| *Incidents* | *Attack* | *Counter Attack!* |
|---|---|---|
| What a big queue! | Red Drunk Monkey | Relax. It happens sometimes |
| Why the hell did she speak like that! | Her Anger Monkey was active due to unmet deadlines. | She is a good person. Give her the benefit of doubt. |
| Slow internet. These people are useless. | Red Drunk Monkey | Can I do something? If not, I need to be patient. |
| No. I can't do it. | Fear Monkey | Feed the monkey with cherries. |
| Let me eat this chocolate one last time. | Beware. P-Monkey is showing up. | Say no. |

| *Incidents* | *Attack* | *Counter Attack!* |
|---|---|---|
| Why is it raining? I was about to leave. | The Complaint Monkey is attacking. | Accept. It's the rainy season and so it will rain. |
| It's too far. I don't want to go. | P-Monkey is coming up! | Reverse engineer. |
| My job sucks. | Miss Grateful is missing. | At least I have one and it was my choice. |
| Just by putting filters on her latest Facebook updates, she thinks she is a queen. | Ego is showing up. | If it gives her happiness, let her do that! |
| Oh no …, it's Monday! | P-Monkey and Complaint Monkey are showing up. | It could mean a fresh start! |
| I don't get paid enough. | Complaint Monkey has hijacked Human Monkey. | Can I do something about that? |
| I put on weight so easily. Whatever I eat, I put on weight. Look at her! | Complaint Monkey and the tendency to compare | Can I do something about that? |
| What traffic! | Complaint Monkey | Can I do something about that? |

| *Incidents* | *Attack* | *Counter Attack!* |
|---|---|---|
| My colleagues are just jealous of me. | Ego Monkey is showing up. | You are probably just overthinking! |
| Last time, he misbehaved. Now its my turn. | Revenge Monkey is popping up. | What I will get after that? |
| The world is stupid. | Judgemental Monkey is showing up. | Let me focus on my work. I am not a judge. |
| Why did she break my heart? I will teach her a lesson. | Beware! Judgemental Monkey is popping up. It will hurt you. | Let me try and analyse why she did this. |
| What has happened in the latest episode of *Game of Thrones*? | P-Monkey is bored and needs some entertainment. | I will watch it once I finish my work. |
| I will do it tomorrow. | P-Monkey is fooling you. | Breathe in. Can I do it now? |
| Don't worry, we have enough time. Let's sleep now. | P-Monkey is fooling you. | Is this the way champions are made? |
| Why should I save money? We should enjoy life. | P-Monkey wants to shop and eat good food. | He is heading towards temporary pleasure and permanent pain. |

| *Incidents* | *Attack* | *Counter Attack!* |
|---|---|---|
| Life is very tough. | Drunk Monkey has taken a sad form. | It's just a phase. |
| I scored very badly in my last test. What if I fail this one? | Wait. Fear Monkey is attacking you and hijacking your confidence. | Use the Candle of Hope. |
| I am very fat. | Complaint Monkey is showing up. | Go to the Purple Island. Focus on what you can do right now. |
| Why did I do so badly in the exams? | Red Drunk Monkey is showing up. | Go to the Purple Island. Focus on what you can do right now. |
| He put ME on hold? | Ego is showing up. | Go to the Purple Island. Focus on what you can do right now. |

# Toolkit

## The Monkey Theory to Reduce Office Stress

1. On the scale of 0-10, what is the stress level you are experiencing?

___

___

2. List down the reasons that shoots up the stress?

___

___

3. Which Monkey is causing the stress?

A. Monkey ☐

B. Fear Monkey ☐

C. Comparison Monkey ☐

D. Ego Monkey ☐

E. Other Monkey ☐

4. Describe how's it troubling you?

---

---

5. Write down any 3 major actions you will take for next one week?

---

---

## The Monkey Theory to Relieve Performance Pressure

(Please tear the page and put it on your working desk)

1. Which Monkey is stressing you?

______________________________________________

______________________________________________

2. Is this Monkey bothering you from childhood?

______________________________________________

______________________________________________

3. Have you tried meditating?

______________________________________________

______________________________________________

4. Is fear of failure bothering you?

______________________________________________

______________________________________________

5. How the scale of 0-10 how much is this Pressure?

______________________________________________

______________________________________________

6. How much winning is important to you?

______________________________________________

______________________________________________

7. Write down 3 actionables which can make you better?

______________________________________________

______________________________________________

8. Take help of breathing techniques to relax, write down your schedule of doing it.

______________________________________________

______________________________________________

## The Monkey Theory to Fight Relationship Stress

1. Which Monkey is causing you stress?

_______________________________________________

_______________________________________________

2. Are you living in the present?

_______________________________________________

_______________________________________________

3. Are you constantly thinking about the incident?

_______________________________________________

_______________________________________________

4. How often you are re-repeating in a day?

_______________________________________________

_______________________________________________

5. Can you take help of Forgiveness Monkey?

_______________________________________________

_______________________________________________

6. What will happen if you forgive this person?

________________________________________

________________________________________

7. Is Ego Monkey damaging it for you?

________________________________________

________________________________________

8. On the scale of 0-10, what's the damage done by Ego Monkey?

________________________________________

________________________________________

9. Write 3 actionables which can free you from the stress?

________________________________________

________________________________________

10. Write a deadline to apply these actionables?

________________________________________

________________________________________

## The Monkey Theory for Self-Acceptance

1. Are you unhappy with something?

2. What is bothering you the most? Which Monkey is responsible for it?

3. Can you change it?

4. How can you change it? If not, how can you accept it?

5. Can you improve your thought process? Take help of Human Monkey to bring discipline?

6. Write 3 Actionables you will for improvement?

## The Monkey Theory to Improve Laziness

1. What is the damage done by P-Monkey? Make a list

___

___

2. What are the trigger points when P-Monkey attacks you?

___

___

3. How can you use Good Fear Monkeys to bring Discipline?

___

___

4. Write 3 New habits to tame P-Monkey?

___

___

5. What you will lose if P-Monkey is not tamed?

___

___